NOTORIOUS GEORGIA

Land Wars, Doc Holliday, the Machetti Murders, and More Historic Crimes

NEELY YOUNG

THE History PRESS

Published by The History Press
An imprint of Arcadia Publishing
Charleston, SC
www.historypress.com

First published 2026

Manufactured in the United States

ISBN 9781467170796

Library of Congress Control Number: 2026942488

I dedicate this book to my loving wife for her understanding and inspiration.

In memory of those who lost their lives.

Yea, though I walk through the valley of the shadow of death, I will fear no evil:
for thou art with me, thy rod and staff they comfort me.
—Psalm 23, Kings James Bible

Alday family:
  Aubrey Alday
  Chester Alday
  Jerry Alday
  Jimmy Alday
  Mary Alday
  Ned Alday
Anderson Prison victims
Cherokee Nation
Gregory and May Dorsey
John C. Forsyth
Leo Frank
Button Gwinnett
Virginia Hill and Benjamin "Bugsy" Siegel
Igbo People
Roger and Dorothy Malcom
Milledgeville's Central Hospital for the Insane Victims
Lemuel Penn
The thirty-one Atlanta child murder victims
Randy Thompson
Glenn Turner
William Turner

CONTENTS

ACKNOWLEDGEMENTS

Thank you to those who gave me help and encouragement while I prepared this book, which documents the most notorious people to have lived and events to have occurred in Georgia.

I am indebted to my associate and friend Heidi Rizzi for her help finishing my project by sending the book to The History Press. In addition, I appreciate Vally Sharpe, who was instrumental in helping me at the early stages of writing and editing this book. I appreciate the editing and production assistance of Cheryl Cromer.

I want to recognize my wonderful wife, Kathy, for giving me advice and encouragement during the many months of writing *Notorious Georgia*.

Lastly, I am always in debt to my special friends who gave me advice when writing my first book, *Georgia Made*, and the many people who have encouraged me to write another book, including Peggy Galis, Micky Blackwell, Frederick Allen, Chad Rhoad with The History Press, my son Benjamin and many others.

INTRODUCTION

Have you ever experienced the horror of having something happen to you that you have no control over? This is a book that tells of vile, evil people who tried to do just that to others and the way sheriffs, judges, and the FBI brought them to justice. Several of these cases went all the way to the Supreme Court.

A few years ago, I lost control of my ability to speak or write. While I lost these abilities, there were people who helped bring me back to my former self.

My experience with this horror started when I received two operations on the left side of my head to correct a benign cancer condition. The result of the operation caused me to lose the ability to speak or write, a condition called *aphasia*. It robs you of the ability to communicate. An example would be mixing up two words like *cemetery* and *seminary*, which one of my friends did when he told his dad he wanted to go into the ministry. His dad was taken aback when his son told him he was going into the cemetery. Then the son said, "I mean the *seminary*." Now, you know the meaning of *aphasia*.

To lose this ability as a journalist was quite a shock. I had to receive major therapy to correct the condition, and I had a wonderful person help me regain the ability to speak. My therapist treated me by asking me to write, as best I could, a document. I would give it back to her to correct and then she would return it and ask me to read it aloud. Over time, my therapist helped me regain the ability to write and speak.

For therapy, I had to find a subject to write about. For many years, I was a journalist and had written columns for newspaper and magazines. In my early days, I was on the police beat and wrote about crime and punishment for my local newspaper. I have always been interested in what makes criminals tick and why they would turn to a life of crime.

Neely Young. *Jennifer Stalcup.*

The stories I have selected for this book are about notorious Georgians from all over the state. They come from many periods and include both men and women.

For example, in 1803, Thomas Spalding and John Couper bought one hundred enslaved Africans named the Igbos. Upon arrival, the Igbos overtook the ship's captain and then dove into the water in what was the largest mass suicide in the history of the slave trade in America. The Igbos repudiated their captivity by choosing death over slavery.

One of the twentieth century's most notorious stories is about Rebecca Machetti, who asked her daughters to hold down their father's legs while she tried to smother him with a pillow. Later, she hired two men to kill him with a shotgun. She was apprehended and sentenced to die in the electric chair, the only woman to ever receive this sentence in Georgia. Later, her sentence was reduced to life in prison. She was described as "a woman whose level of wickedness spared no one, not even her own daughters."

Even in sports, evil can be found. Ty Cobb was a professional baseball player in the mid-twentieth century. While he was one the best players in history, he was hated by his fellow players. He was known as the meanest player in baseball. He wore spikes in his shoes to hurt other players, and one time, he pistol-whipped a man simply for crossing the street in front of him. Yet when he died, he donated money to start a hospital to treat poor farmers near his home in Royston.

The history of moonshine tells the stories of poor families in the mountains of Georgia making tax-free corn whiskey and driving it down to Atlanta to sell. One man, Eli Field, found a way to fight tax revenuers. He called his organization the "Honest Man's Friend and Protector Group." Field's company became a violent crime and vigilante gang that terrorized any informant who worked with the revenuers. It became a war, and federal troops were brought in to stop the conflict. Over the years, agents and moonshiners became friends, built dirt tracks, and raced their cars down the mountains to see which was the fastest. This was the birth of modern-day NASCAR.

In 1913, Georgia Governor John Slaton condemned Leo Frank, the man who was sentenced to hang for the murder of thirteen-year-old Mary Phagan. The governor offered no reason for Frank to be spared hanging for the crime but changed his sentence to life in prison. Great evilness followed. The governor was hounded out of office and had to flee to another state.

One of the more horrible stories is that of Carl Isaac and the Alday Murders. On a dark day in Southwest Georgia, Isaac and his gang of escaped prisoners killed six members of a fine family, farmers who were trying to get their crops ready for market.

Lynn Turner convinced her husband to take out a life insurance policy and later killed him by serving him Jell-O laced with antifreeze. She then got a new boyfriend to take out a policy—and then served him poisoned Jell-O as well. When he died, she tried to cash in. The media dubbed the case the "Jell-O Murders."

This book is not meant to be a work of scholarship; instead, it is a list of the horrors of those who were vile and considered crazy and how federal and state authorities tracked them down and brought them to justice. Not all the culprits were found, but the effort was made and we should be proud of the lawmakers of our state who helped keep us safe.

They will be remembered collectively as leaders to the cause of law and order in the march of Georgia history.

1
THE ALDAY MURDERS

The Dark Day Escaped Prisoners Killed Six Members of a South Georgia Family

May 14, 1973, was a dark day in Donalsonville, a small city in Seminole County near the Alabama line in Southwest Georgia. The area is known for growing peanuts, cotton, and corn.

Six members of the Alday family had a farm on Spooner Road, south of town. The family was well known and highly respected in the community. They used a trailer as their home base during crop planting time. When they arrived at their trailer that day for a summer meal, they had no idea of the horror that was awaiting them.

Four escaped prisoners from Maryland were lying in wait. That afternoon, the four fugitives murdered Ned Alday, sixty-two; Jerry Alday, thirty-four; Jimmy Alday, twenty-four; Mary Alday, twenty-five; Chester "Snuggie" Alday, thirty; and Aubrey Alday, fifty. The four young men who carried out this senseless act were Carl Isaac, Wayne Coleman, George Dundee, and Billy Isaac.

Carl Isaac was living in Maryland when he was arrested for stealing and sent to Maryland's Poplar Hill Prison Camp. His half brother Wayne Coleman was already at the facility. Carl found Wayne and told him he had an escape plan. Wayne wanted to be included, as did a friend, George Dundee. The three escaped through a bathroom window and then stole a car. Carl decided to pick up his little brother, Billy Isaac. The men stole another car from a man in Pennsylvania, and when the man fought the four of them, Carl killed him and dumped his body in the woods by his home.

Missing Woman Found Slain, Sixth Victim in Georgia Family

Killers Strike At Mobile Home

By MIKE CHRISTENSEN and CHARLES WHEELER

Six members of a Seminole County farm family were murdered Monday night or early Tuesday by unknown assailants who are believed to have fled in an automobile owned by one of the victims.

Officials identified the dead as Ned Alday, 65; his brother, Aubrey, 57; Ned's three sons: Jerry, 35; Chester, 32, and Jimmy, 25, and Ned's wife Mary, in her 20s.

The five men were discovered by a relative at 2:15 a.m. Tuesday in a two-bedroom mobile home off a rural road about 10 miles south of Donalsonville near the Chattahoochee River, officials said.

The body of Ned's wife was located Tuesday morning about four miles from the trailer, the state patrol said.

A spokesman for the state patrol said the woman apparently had been dumped by the side of a road. No other details were immediately available.

Mrs. Alday had at first been reported missing, along with the car, a 1970 Chevrolet Impala, dark blue with a white top, and bearing Georgia tag number MIY 519.

The men in the mobile home were all shot to death, officials said. Two of the men were found in each of the mobilehome's two bedrooms. The fifth victim was discovered on a couch in the living room.

The home is located a half-mile from Ned Alday's home, focal point of the family's large corn, cotton and hog farm.

Authorities said they have no word on possible suspects in the mass killings, and no motive.

DESCRIBING the scene, Seminole County Sheriff Dan White said there were no signs of a struggle, and none of the victims were bound.

A sheriff's department spokesman said the bodies were found by a relative Ray Alday, who went to the scene after wives of the victims became worried.

Aubrey Alday, one of the

Staff Photo—Bill Wilson

STEVE SANDIFORD CHECKS BOARD FOR CLOSED CIRCUIT TV MONITORS
Cameras Installed Around At Shafts on Each Floor of Baptist Towers

Atlanta Journal, May 15, 1973.

Their plan was drive to Florida and lay low. The four were driving through South Georgia and needed gas and food. They were driving south near Donalsonville when they saw a gas tank and mobile home, so they stopped and broke into the trailer looking for food.

Then Ned Alday and his son Jerry pulled up. Carl forced them into the trailer at gunpoint and robbed them. Then they were taken to the bedrooms in the back of the home. Carl Isaac shot Jerry in the head four times. Wayne Coleman shot Ned in the head. When Ned fought Coleman, Carl Isaacs shot him five more times.

Jimmy Alday drove up on his tractor, and Carl forced him inside. Jimmy was forced onto a couch and shot by Carl twice in the back of his head. Then Jerry's wife, Mary, arrived. Carl crept up behind her and forced her inside the trailer. Mary was sitting at the dining table when Chester and Aubrey Alday arrived. Carl brought them into the house at gunpoint. Chester was taken back to the bedroom, where Wayne Coleman shot him. Carl Isaacs took Aubrey into the same room and killed him.

Mary Alday was raped by two of the men. The four then took her car and drove her to a secluded area, where they raped her again. During the rape, the men took pictures. Afterward, George Dundee murdered her.

Instead of going to Florida to escape the crime scene, the four killers drove Mary's car north to West Virginia. They were caught four days later and sent back to Seminole County, where they were arrested. Six counts of murder were read to each of the men by the county's district attorney.

The citizens of Donalsonville and Seminole County were shocked by the brutal murders of the Aldays. They were much beloved, and their massacre was a devastating loss. The media attention was intense. The local newspaper, the *Early County News*, the *Albany Herald*, and local TV stations from the area carried details of the killings. Both the *Atlanta Journal* and the *Atlanta Constitution* and the national media covered the trial.

In January 1974, all four men were tried by a jury in Donalsonville. The prosecutor for the trial was former Lieutenant Governor Peter Zack Geer. During the trial, Geer asked the jury to "use [your] Georgia walking sense and tell me if Carl Isaac has an abandoned and malignant heart."

The jury took only thirty-eight minutes to produce a verdict. When the judge asked the foreman for the verdict, he answered, "Guilty as charged."

Billy Isaac agreed to cooperate with the prosecutors and received a twenty-year sentence for armed robbery. Carl Isaacs, Wayne Coleman, and George Dundee, however, were convicted of murder and sentenced to be executed by lethal injection.

Before the four were arrested, reporters had interviewed Sheriff Dan White, who said, "If I had my way about it, I'd have me a large oven, and I'd precook [the suspects] for several days."

The three appealed their sentences to higher courts but were rejected due "to the overwhelming incontrovertible evidence of their willful participation

Six in Family Are Slain In Seminole 'Execution'

By SAM HOPKINS
Constitution Staff Writer

DONALSONVILLE — Six members of a well-known Seminole County farming family were shot to death "execution style" in what one official Tuesday called "The biggest deliberately planned homicide in Georgia."

A three-state alert was issued for four suspects, three of them work camp escapees from Maryland believed to have stolen a car in Pennsylvania.

The six victims included two brothers, three grown sons of one of the brothers and the wife of one of the sons.

The five slain men, all shot in the head, were discovered several hours after midnight in the trailer home of one of the sons, Jerry Alday, after other members of the family reported them missing.

Officials identified the dead as brothers Ned and Aubrey Alday, both in their 50s; Ned Alday's three sons, Jerry, 33, Chester, [illegible], and Jimmy, [illegible], and Jerry's wife, Mary, 25.

Mrs. Alday and the family car were missing when the bodies of the five men were discovered. Her body was found shortly after noon Tuesday in a field about six miles north of the Alday farm.

All of the Alday families farmed together on a 525-acre tract of land they owned

12,000 Years in Prison Given to 2 in Texas

SAN ANTONIO, Tex. (UPI) — A jury Tuesday sentenced a man convicted of killing a policeman to 2,000 years in prison. The day before, a judge issued a 10,000-year prison term to another man convicted of killing an officer.

Despite the length of the sentences, the two men will be eligible for parole in 20 years.

A jury of 10 men and two women deliberated two and one-half hours before sentencing John L. Harris, 26, to 2,000 years for the murder of San Antonio policeman George Jacobs last Jan. 10.

On Monday, district Judge Archie S. Brown sentenced Eugene Spencer Jr., 27, to 10,000 years in prison for killing patrolman Antonio T. Canales on May 8, 1972.

CHECK 'KITE'

Tellers'

Atlanta Constitution, May 16, 1973.

in what is generally regarded as the most heinous criminal orgy in the history of the state."

Ten years later, in 1985, the United States Court of Appeals for the Eleventh Circuit overturned all three death convictions and sentences and ordered new trials. The court agreed that there was "overwhelming evidence" of the defendants' guilt, but it also agreed with the defendants' contentions in their appeals that there was "overwhelming evidence that the community had prejudiced both guilt and sentence." The court stated that the pretrial coverage in the media, both locally and nationally, as well comments like those of Sheriff White, prejudiced the jury. The court stated that if it did not overturn the defendants' convictions, "an obviously guilty defendant would have a right to a fair trial."

Later, the U.S. Supreme Court upheld the lower court's decision to hold a new trial.

In 1988, Carl Isaac's retrial was held in Perry, a small town only one hundred miles from Donalsonville. Community leaders in Perry were worried about potential violence that could be taken against Isaac, so they posted extra security around the trial. Isaac was again found guilty and sentenced to death. After he had exhausted all his appeals, Isaac was executed by lethal injection on May 6, 2003. He had lived on death row for thirty years.

On May 2, 1988, Wayne Coleman's retrial was held in DeKalb County. Coleman was again convicted for the murders of the Aldays. But the jury could not agree to send Coleman to the electric chair, so the judge sentenced him to six consecutive life sentences.

George Dundee's retrial was scheduled to occur in Columbus but was never held because Dundee pleaded guilty. Prosecutors were unable to seek the death sentence due to Dundee's "significantly sub-average general intellectual functions." The judge imposed six life sentences, with the understanding that Dundee would never be paroled.

In 2025, the *Early County News* published a story, "The Alday Murders: Southwest Georgia's Darkest Day Marks 50 Years." The editor's note reads, "May we never forget Seminole County's tragic loss of the Alday family, the reality of evil and the promise from Almighty God that He will exact vengeance."

2

BUTTON GWINNETT

The Most Notorious Signer of the Declaration of Independence

Button Gwinnett, Dr. Lyman George Hall, and George Watson were the three Georgians who signed the Declaration of Independence in 1776. They were heroic men—save for one. Button Gwinnett failed the test to be called a hero, but he might have had the last laugh.

Georgia played a minor role in the adoption of the concept of revolution against England. It was the only colony to agree with the Stamp Act and did not send anyone to the First Continental Congress. Those in Georgia who opposed the English were out-of-power planters, merchants, and rural farmers from the backwoods. This last faction was the group Button Gwinnett was set to lead.

One way to describe Gwinnett is that he was *feckless*, meaning he was incompetent, irresponsible, and ineffectual. So, he was always in trouble with creditors. In the 1760s, he left England and brought his family to Charleston, South Carolina, where he became a merchant. In this endeavor, he failed. To escape bankruptcy, in 1765, he moved to Savannah, where he failed in every endeavor he tried. One reason for his failures is that he was a difficult person to deal with: He always feuded with others, and most people stayed away from him.

After he failed to become a merchant, Gwinnett borrowed money to purchase a plantation on St. Catherine's Island, which included enslaved laborers. This venture failed when Gwinnett's creditor refused to extend his loan. The people who loaned him the money described him as a "chronic debtor," and he was forced to sell the plantation.

Button Gwinnett, signer of the Declaration of Independence. *University of Georgia Press.*

Gwinnett retreated to a rural township south of Savannah and soon became involved in politics. In 1775, revolution fever was a hot topic in the colonies, and Gwinnett began organizing residents in the small towns to become involved in the movement. He formed a group to oppose Savannah's citizens who might want to control local political events.

The Continental Congress was a way to form a new government for those who wanted to separate from England. They sent a regiment of troops to Georgia to protect the citizens poised to force England to abandon Savannah. Gwinnett tried to win the appointment as colonel of the regiment; he won the rural vote, but Savannah's elite refused to appoint him. Gwinnett did, however, win the election to become one of Georgia's members of the Continental Congress. There, he served on a committee to study how the new country could form a government.

When the Declaration of Independence was ready, Gwinnett, Hall, and Walton arrived in Philadelphia just in time to sign it. They were there to enjoy the celebrations and a public dinner and to see citizens hold a funeral to symbolically "bury the British government."

Back in Savannah, Gwinnett became president and commander-in-chief of Georgia's military forces. Gwinnett was riding high when he received a letter from Congress accusing him of misappropriating funds intended for Georgia. He kept the accusation from others and burned the letter.

The newly appointed general of the army in the Savannah area was Lachlan McIntosh. Gwinnett sent McIntosh a letter stating that he, as president—not McIntosh—was the principal leader of all military forces in Georgia. This letter became the cause of a great feud between Gwinnett and Lachlan and Lachan's brother George that later had terrible consequences for Gwinnett.

Gwinnett decided to invade British St. Augustine, founded in Florida. He asked General Robert Howe, the commander of the southern army, for more troops to aid in the invasion. Howe considered the mission a fool's folly but sent a small attachment to Savannah. Gwinnett said, "He came, he saw and left us in low estate."

Gwinnett went on with has invasion without consulting McIntosh. The assault on St. Augustine was a disaster, with Gwinnett and McIntosh pointing fingers at each for the defeat. The strong jealousies between the two intensified.

Lachlan's brother George was accused of having business dealings with people who favored the king and British interests. Gwinnett had George arrested, charged with treason, and jailed. Gwinnett refused him bail, even though McIntosh had no way to determine what charges had been brought against him. Gwinnett even refused to allow George a trial in Georgia.

Gwinnett left Savannah on business, and when he came back, he was surprised to find that he had been replaced by a new president (governor) and commander-in-chief, John Adam Treutlen.

Later, the Georgia Council of Safety voted to release McIntosh, pending his available time to prepare a defense for a trial. On May 8, 1777, at his trial, the jury found George guilty. After hearing the verdict, Lachlan called Gwinnett "a scoundrel and a lying rascal."

Gwinnett was embarrassed to be called this in front of the entire assembly and quickly challenged Lachlan to a duel. Tradition held that for a duel to be successful, both participants would compel only the requirement of honor rather than take each other's lives. The two men met in a park north of the city. Dr. George Wells served as Gwinnett's second, a man to help if Lachlan's shot hit its mark and killed him. Joseph Habersham acted as Lachlan's second. As was custom, each challenger began the duel standing back to back. Normally, the two would have walked fifteen to twenty feet before turning to fire, but both were in a hurry to get the duel over with and requested the distance be set at ten feet. As they turned, the two shot each other in the legs, not in a way that would kill the other. After they left the field and went back to their homes, the seconds on both sides reported that the event was harmless and was successful, as the two had solved their quarrel in an honorable way.

Gwinnett was brought to his home and helped to his bed. His wife was upset because she thought the two should have been separated by twenty feet, as was custom. He was attended by a local doctor, and his leg was bandaged. The bandage became infected, however, and on the morning of May 19, Gwinnett died, only eight months after he signed the Declaration of Independence. Despite his many faults, Gwinnett is remembered as one of the founders of our country.

Lachlan McIntosh turned himself in to the court and was charged with murder, but he was acquitted at trial. He later left Georgia and served under General George Washington until the end of the American Revolution.

A congressional committee was later formed, which found Gwinnett had stolen government moneys. His properties were auctioned off to repay what was owed.

In 1778, British troops easily captured Savannah and returned Georgia back to the Crown. History records that it was Gwinnett's ambitious and controversial actions that resulted in the disaster. One official recorded, "Gwinnett appears to be a man of many talents, but he was hasty in his decisions, overbearing in his temper, and wild and reckless in his plans."

In the last part of the twentieth century, citizens in Savannah created a park named the Colonial Cemetery to honor all those Georgians who were part of the Revolutionary War. Although they were able to find the grave sites of other contributors and place markers of distinction for them, they were unable to find Gwinnett's grave, despite searching diligently. Finally, several years later, they came upon an unmarked spot that looked like a grave site. Because the body's left leg bone was fractured, they decided it was Gwinnett's. With great ceremony, they honored him as one of the Georgians who signed the Declaration of Independence.

There are many people who collect the signatures of those who signed the Declaration of Independence, and Button Gwinnett's autograph is the rarest of them all. There is much interest from collectors who want a complete set of the fifty-six signers, and there are only a few of his signatures available. His autograph could be worth over a $1 million in today's market, according to Christie's Auction House.

Several Georgia counties have been named for those who took part in these events. Hall County is named for Lyman Hall. Walton County is named for George Walton. McIntosh County is named for Lachlan McIntosh. Habersham County is named for Joseph Habersham. Treutlen County is named for John Adam Treutlen. And the second-largest county in Georgia, with over one million residents, is named Gwinnett County after Button Gwinnett, one of the founding fathers of our country.

3

RESURGENCE OF THE KU KLUX KLAN

The Killing of Lemuel Penn by the Klan and the 1964 Trial of the Killers Howard Sims and Cecil William Myers

Formed after Civil War, the Ku Klux Klan (KKK) was an organization designated, in its stance, to protect white people and advocate against federal influences during Reconstruction. The second Klan was formed in 1915 by William Simons, who designed a costume of white robes and hoods to hide the faces of Klan members. He climbed Stone Mountain and burned a large cross—the Klan's symbol based on an ancient Scottish tradition in which a burning wooden cross was passed among a clan to declare war. His goal was to promote white supremacy and protect the rights of white Americans against Black Americans and other minorities.

The Ku Klux Klan's membership, at its highest, was more than 5 million nationwide in the 1920s, with more than 150,000 members in Georgia. But by the 1940s, the state's membership had declined to fewer than 1,400 members.

But the Klan was far from dead. An Atlanta physician, Samuel Green, formed the Association of Georgia Klans, which emphasized anticommunism and violence against Blacks.

In 1954, in the case of *Brown v. Board of Education*, the U.S. Supreme Court ruled that separating children in public schools based on race was unconstitutional. Georgia's political leaders rebelled. Governor Marvin Griffin changed the state's flag to include the Stars and Bars of the old Confederate flag. The next governor, Lester Maddox, was famous for displaying axe handles in his restaurant as a threat to Black people who might to try to visit his establishment.

Broad River Bridge plaque. *Plaque from the Georgia Historical Society.*

The KKK soon returned to its old mission of violence and terror against Black Americans. In 1955, the Knights of the Ku Klux Klan walked up Stone Mountain to stage a rally, with three thousand in attendance. This new group was highly organized, with targeted attacks against Black Americans and supporters of the civil rights movement. The Klan was a still small group in the state at the time, but it had become influential, as politicians and other citizens had remained active during the 1950s and '60s.

In 1964, President Lyndon B. Johnson signed the Voting Rights Act, a landmark law that prohibited racial discrimination in voting. Demonstrations against the law were held in Georgia, and Klan activity increased.

On July 11, 1964, just nine days after the signing of the act, three Black World War II veterans were driving home from Fort Benning. Lemuel Penn, a former lieutenant colonel in the Army Reserves, was at the wheel. Penn had seen combat in the South Pacific and remained active in the army. In 1939, he became a high school teacher and taught for twenty years in the District of Columbia system. He rose to become assistant superintendent in charge of vocational and adult education for Washington, D.C.'s five vocational schools. He was an influential man in his community, active in the First Methodist church and the Boy Scouts, where he won the Silver Beaver Award, the scout's highest leadership honor. His wife was a home economics teacher in her community high school. They had three children. The other men with him, Charles E. Brown and John D. Howard, were from his hometown and had finished their assignments at Fort Benning. They decided to take a shortcut when they left Athens and drove up a two-land road to Hartwell, where they planned to connect to I-85 North. They did not notice a Chevrolet station wagon following about one hundred yards behind them.

The Chevy started closing in on them and moved into the left lane. Penn's car drove over the bridge to the Broad River. The station wagon pulled up beside them. There were two loud explosions. Penn's car swerved and hit the bridge rail. Brown saw that Penn was slumped over the steering wheel and grabbed the wheel to get the car under control. He noticed that Penn was badly hurt, and when he looked again, he saw that Penn was dead. The shotgun had taken the front his head off. The second shot was aimed at Brown but had missed.

The men in the other car were members of the Athens Ku Klux Klan. Joseph Howard Sims, Herbert Guest, James S. Lackey, and Cecil William Myers saw Penn's car had a Washington, D.C. tag and thought the three were civil rights agitators looking for trouble. The real reason they targeted the men was because they were Black.

A local police officer, Billy Smith, and another man were driving to the bridge when they saw Brown on the highway, waving his arms and yelling that they were in trouble. Smith examined the car and saw Penn's body. He called Madison County Sheriff Dewy Seagraves, who sent Brown, Howard, and the body of Penn back to Athens.

Sheriff Seagraves notified the FBI of Penn's slaying. Several agents of the bureau, including Jack Simpson and Joseph Ponder, were called in to help with the investigation. While the local sheriff oversaw the investigation, he was aware that the crime would have national significance. The sheriff also notified the Criminal Investigation Division of the Army Military Police.

After a manhunt that lasted a month or longer, all three perpetrators were arrested and charged with the crime. Sims was a machinist and a father of eight children. He had a been with the Klan for many years and was known for carrying out acts of violence in Athens. Guest was a 282-pound garage operator who kept shotguns in the back window of his car. Myers was a yarn picker. He was a proud Klansman and wore a pistol on his hip during the day. Lackey was gas pumper at Peoples Gas service station in Athens.

A grand jury was seated, and indictments were returned against Myers, Sims, and Lackey. Guest was charged as an accessory, but he was not indicted. Lackey confessed to the crime but was not charged.

On August 31, 1964, the trial of Sims and Myers for the murder of Penn opened in the Madison County Courthouse. Governor Carl Sanders was interested in the case and appointed Jeff Wayne as special prosecutor. Local prosecutor Crete Johnson joined him. John Darsey and James Hudson represented Sims and Myers.

Wayne and Johnson thought they had an airtight case that would convict Sims and Myers. Lackey had already confessed to the crime. All they needed to do was put Lackey on the stand and have him testify to what the killers had done to Penn.

Johnson read the confession, in part, to the jury:

> *On the morning of July 11, 1964, I was driving Cecil Myers' cream Chevy station wagon accompanied by Cecil Myers and Howard Sims. At some time between 4 a.m. and 4:30 a.m., we spotted a 1959 Chevy occupied by several colored men. We trailed the car and noticed the Washington, D.C. plates. I was driving, and I began following the car, as directed by Myers. Sims told me to fall back and follow the Negroes, and I stayed back about one or two hundred yards. I asked the others what they were going to do and Sims said, "I'm going to kill me a* [Black man]*." Myers said he would help Sims.*
>
> *Both Sims and Myers told me when to pass the car occupied by Negroes from Washington D.C. When I was alongside the Negroes' car, both Sims and Myers fired shotguns into the Negroes' car.*

The defense team, led by Hudson, tried to discredit Lackey. They said that Lackey had repudiated his confession. On the stand, Sims said, "I am innocent of the killing of Lemuel Penn. I understand that the act happened around 5 o'clock in the morning of July 11, and I was in Athens at that time."

Darcy addressed the jury and, in an emotional closing, railed against the federal government. He roared at the "carpetbagging administration of justice" and the FBI, which had swarms of agents who "infiltrated our land."

The jury began deliberating the case, and at 10:00 p.m., they told the judge they had reached a verdict. As Sims and Myers waited anxiously, the clerk read, "We, the jury, find the defendants, Joseph Howard Sims and Cecil Myers, not guilty."

The defense was assured a victory because, it was discovered, the jury was packed with Klansmen. On the night after the verdict was read, the Ku Klux Klan held a rally at Stone Mountain to celebrate. They wore their white uniforms and burned a giant cross. Grand Wizard James Venable declared, "You'll never be able to convict a white man that killed a [Black man] that encroached on the white race in the South."

Sims and Myers were heroes of the KKK. They appeared at Klan rallies all over the South. They took part in cross burnings at the homes of Black Americans. Lester Maddox, who was soon elected governor of Georgia, praised the two as symbols of states' rights. At one of the rallies, Sheriff Dewey Seagraves attended, wearing a Klan uniform.

But as a noted sportswriter once said, "Not so fast."

The Department of Justice wanted to prosecute the three on the federal level. On October 16, 1964, a grand jury indicted them using the recently enacted Civil Rights Act of 1964. In this second trial, the jury found Sims and Myers guilty of killing Penn. Judge Willam Bootle sentenced them to ten years in the federal penitentiary.

Most Southerners were not supportive of the KKK. They were in favor of Martin L. King Jr. and his fight for equal rights, and they despised the Ku Klux Klan and what it believed. After the trial of Myers and Sims, Klan groups began to disband. Grand Dragon George Calvin resigned his position. He later joined the Atlanta Model Cities Program, which worked to bring Black and white residents together. Across Georgia, people of color and white people worked together to bring about the integration of schools, retail establishments, and government facilities. The Ku Klux Klan did rise again in other situations but was never as powerful as it once had been.

Those who asked for justice for Lemuel Penn knew that he was killed for two reasons: His car had a Washington, D.C. plate, and he was a Black man. He will be remembered by those who loved him for his influence in the cause of civil rights, even after his death.

Editor's note: This story comes from the book The Murder at Broad River Bridge: The Slaying of Lemuel Penn by the Ku Klux Klan, *by Bill Shipp. Shipp was a close friend of mine and a great advocate for equal rights for all Americans. He became a famous editor of the* Atlanta Journal-Constitution *and wrote about politics and the fight for equality for Black Americans. This book was written in 1981. Ship was vilified by members of the KKK, but he survived and was selected as a member of the Hall of Fame of authors in the state of Georgia.*

4

TY COBB

The Meanest Man in Baseball

Ty Cobb was a professional baseball player in the early twentieth century. He was considered one the best baseball players of the time. Named the "Georgia Peach" by his fans, he was also controversial due to his fearsome, aggressive playing style.

Cobb was born in Narrows and grew up in Royston. He was the son of William and Amanda Cobb. As a child, he became fascinated with baseball and told his father he wanted to be a professional baseball player. His father was opposed to Cobb's wishes. His father was a violent man and told Cobb, "Don't come home a failure."

William Cobb believed his wife was having an affair with another man. He spied on Amanda by standing outside her window, trying to catch her with another man. She heard someone outside her window and, thinking it was an intruder, shot William dead. Amanda was charged with murder but was acquitted because the jury felt she acted in self-defense.

Three weeks after his mother killed his father, Ty Cobb was drafted by the Detroit Tigers. He was only eighteen years old at the time, the youngest player in the league. As a newcomer, he was unpopular with his veteran teammates, and they subjected him to severe hazing. Cobb later attributed his hostile behavior to his future teammates to his treatment in his early years.

Cobb had a burning desire to win every game he played. "I never could stand losing," he said. "Second place did not interest me."

Ty Cobb, baseball legend. *Public domain.*

Cobb played for the Tigers for twenty-two years and later played for the Philadelphia Athletics. He was known for his aggressive base running and once used sharp spikes on his shoes to hurt the other team's players. He won nine consecutive American League batting titles from 1907 to 1915 and hit .320 for consecutive seasons. In 1909, Cobb led the league in home runs and won the Triple Crown. In 1911, he led the American League in every category, including hits, runs, RBI, batting average, and slugging percentage. He was named the league's Most Value Player. For twenty-two consecutive years, he hit .320, including .400 three times. His career stats include 3,034 games played, 4,189 hits, 2,245 runs, 117 home runs, 1,944 RBIs, and 897 stolen bases.

Hall of Fame manager Casey Stengel said of Cobb, "I have never seen anyone like Ty Cobb. No one was even close to him. He was the greatest all-time ball player. The guy was superhuman, amazing." George Sisler, Cobb's fellow Hall of Famer, said, "The greatness of Ty Cobb was something that had to be seen, and to see him was to remember him forever."

Cobb was also known as the meanest man in baseball. He was disliked by teammates and was known as someone who thought nothing of injuring his fellow players just to reach another base or score a run.

Cobb and fellow player Sam Crawford carried on a fearless rivalry. Crawford played alongside Cobb in the outfield. Crawford was a great player and was one of the best sluggers of his era, leading in home runs, runs batted in, and triples. The two never spoke to each other. In retirement, Cobb wrote a letter to a sportswriter accusing Crawford of not helping in the outfield. Crawford read the letter and replied that Cobb was a "cheapskate" who never helped his teammates. Crawford said that Cobb had never been a good fielder and that his letter was wrong about him not helping Cobb in the outfield—he insisted Cobb had "dreamed that up."

After Cobb's death in 1961, a man named Al Stump authored several books about him. Stump wrote that when children wrote Cobb asking for an autographed picture, Cobb would steam the stamps off the return envelopes and never write back. One author, Timothy Gay, wrote that Cobb would pistol-whip any Black man he saw on the street. Cobb, it was said, had an extremely thin skin, and fought with Black and white men alike.

When he retired, Cobb was a wealthy man. He became generous and donated $100,000 in his parent's names for his hometown to build a modern, twenty-four-bed hospital, Cobb Memorial Hospital, now part of the Ty Cobb Health System. He also established the Cobb Educational Fund, endowing it with $100,000 (equivalent to approximately $1,175,249 today). The fund awards scholarships to needy Georgians who are ready for college.

Ty Cobb died in July 1961 at the age of seventy-four. After a small, brief service, he was buried in his family's mausoleum in Royston. He had a great legacy in baseball, and his contributions to help young people go to college was something he was most proud of. Yet many players felt he was trying to buy himself into heaven. The players he abused or hurt with his spikes always felt he was the meanest man in baseball.

5

CHARLES LAMAR

A Civil War "Blacker" and Slave Trader and the Last Man Killed in the Civil War

A *Blacker* is a moniker used in the Bible that, during the 1800s, was used to describe someone who was a vile, immoral, or a cheat. Charles Augustus Lafayette Lamar aptly fit this description. He was a "fire-eating" radical who wanted no restrictions on importing enslaved people into the United States.

Born in Savannah in 1824, Lamar grew up in a wealthy family of bankers and plantation owners. In June 1938, he lost many of his family members in the *Pulaski* disaster, in which a ship's boiler exploded and sank the vessel, killing 128. Out of the 10 members of his immediate family, only 4 survived, including Lamar, his father, and 2 siblings.

In 1846, Lamar married Caroline Agnes Nicoll, the daughter of Judge John Nicoll. He settled in Savannah and opened a grocery store and other businesses. When the store failed in 1844, he took over his father's business, which included a large wharf on the Savannah River.

In 1855, Lamar became a city council member, but when his term ended, he failed to be reelected. He was a difficult person to work with and was once arrested for fighting in the street. In another dispute over a horse race, he shot one of his friends.

After incurring serious debts due to bad investments in gold mining, Lamar turned to a life of crime, illegal slave trading. The importation of enslaved people had been banned since 1808. The enslaved people who were already in America at the time were able to legally remain. Lamar bought a ship, the *E.A. Rawlings*, and remodeled it to import a cargo of enslaved people. He hired a ship captain and ordered him to sail to the coast of

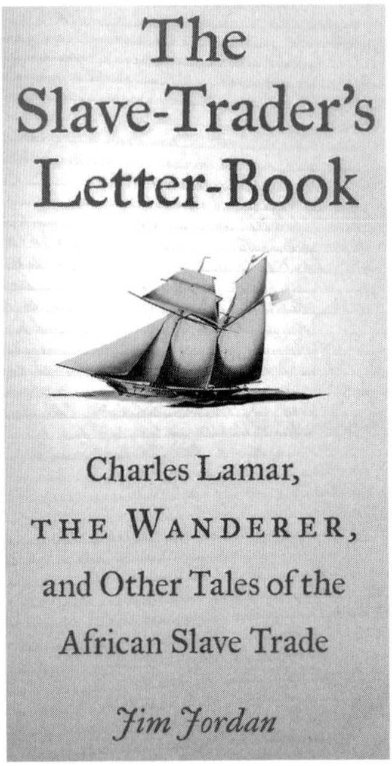

Tales of the slave ship *Wanderer*. *University of Georgia Press.*

Africa, purchase enslaved laborers, return to Savannah, and bypass port officials to reach the slave market. The ship's living cargo was hidden in the hull. But the captain was afraid of being caught with the illegal cargo and avoided Savannah. Instead, he sailed to New Orleans. The captain then sold the enslaved people and kept the money. Lamar lost his investment in the venture.

Lamar's next voyage to Africa came in 1858. The *E.A. Rawlings* landed in Cuba and unloaded a large cargo of enslaved people. But when the ship returned to Savannah, it was seized by federal authorities. Lamar's business plans kept losing money.

His money problems continued to plague him, so he made another attempt to operate an illegal slave trade operation. He wanted to use another ship, the *Richard Cobden*, to sail to Africa and buy enslaved people. But court officials, knowing Lamar's reputation, denied all three of his applications to sail to Africa. They correctly thought it was a ruse to secretly import enslaved laborers to the United States. Lamar's cousin was Howell Cobb, the government official who approved sailing applications. Lamar, always a hot head, issued a letter in newspapers that criticized and insulted Cobb, even though he would need Cobb's approval for any future action.

Lamar became desperate. He obtained a group of investors to lead an expedition on a ship called the *Wanderer*. His plan was to avoid inspection by operating the ship as a pleasure yacht. This time, it passed inspection and departed the Savannah harbor in the summer of 1858. Captain William R. Corrie sailed the ship to the Belgium Congo, where the investors purchased 487 enslaved Africans. The ship was outfitted with large, empty water tanks to use for transporting its cargo; 80 enslaved people died on the trip back to America.

On November 29, the *Wanderer* arrived at Jekyll Island off the coast of Georgia. In what was a collection of many serious mistakes, Lamar had failed to hire a local pilot to help bring the ship into the harbor. Captain Corrie had to go ashore to hire a pilot and had to disclose the investor's plans. After the cargo was taken off the ship and housed in makeshift cabins, Lamar and his business associates traveled to Jekyll Island, where they distributed the enslaved laborers to plantations across the South.

In another mistake, Lamar failed to sign clearance for the *Wanderer* to sail to other ports on the Eastern Seaboard. This raised further suspicions from other authorities.

Rumors of the ship landing at the Jekyll Island came to the editors of Savannah's newspapers, who started writing stories about illegal slave trading in the area. The federal attorney for Georgia, Joseph Galahi, read the stories and began collecting evidence against Lamar. When the *Wanderer* entered Savannah, Galahi had the captain and crew arrested and the ship seized. The ship was later used by the North as a gunboat and a hospital ship. After the Civil War, it sank in the Caribbean Sea during a storm. Historians believe it was the last ship to bring enslaved people to Georgia.

The news about the arrests of Lamar and his men and the illegal smuggling of enslaved people spread nationwide. Lamar's father-in-law, Judge Nicoll, ordered that the ship be auctioned off, since it had been used for slave trading.

In November 1859 and May 1860, several trials were held, and five members of the crew were tried for piracy. Lamar and his associates were charged with holding enslaved Africans who had been trafficked. Lamar was difficult and argumentative during the trial. He even challenged a witness to a duel. He was involved in a jailbreak to free the crew. He was arrested several times but beat the charges because the jury found him not guilty. Most of the other charges were dropped due to Georgia's secession from the Union.

At the beginning of the Civil War, Lamar organized the 7th Georgia Battalion, which became part of the 61st Infantry. He joined the army and became the lieutenant colonel responsible for the defense of Jekyll Island. He resigned his commission in 1862 and started a business supplying the Confederate states with food and arms. His major responsibility was buying ships to organize blockade running for the South.

Near the end of the war, after General William Tecumseh Sherman's March to the Sea, Lamar re-enlisted in the Confederate army and was stationed in Columbus. In 1865, he fought there in what was the last battle of the Civil War.

Charles Augustus Lafayette Lamar, age forty-one, was killed by a stray bullet during the battle. He was buried at the famous Laurel Grove Cemetery in Savannah. He was known for his involvement in slave trading and piracy and for being the last officer killed in the American Civil War.

6

HENRY WIRZ

A Confederate Captain Commanding the Prison at Fort Sumter, Where Thirteen Thousand Union Prisoners Died

During the last part of the Civil War, Henry Wirz, a Confederate army captain, commanded the Union prison in Andersonville. He was arrested, tried, convicted, and sentenced to hang as the only war criminal in the Civil War due to how he handled the deaths of more than thirteen thousand prisoners in the camp over a fourteen-month period. But was he guilty or a scapegoat?

In 1864, Wirz came to live near Americus, where the prison was located in Southwest Georgia. He had an unusual history before he became the head of the prison system. Wirz was born in Switzerland in 1822 and later studied to become a doctor. His field of focus was homeopathic medicine, and he was assigned to a hospital near the Swiss border of Italy, where he was later dismissed because of his controversial methods of patient care. He immigrated to the United States in 1848, settling in New York City as a homeopathic physician. Wirz moved to other locations, including Connecticut and Massachusetts, before he settled in Kentucky. In 1857, Levin R. Marshall employed Wirz to run his 2,200-acre plantation in Louisiana, Cabin Teele. He oversaw hundreds of enslaved workers and ran plantation operations.

At the beginning of the Civil War, Wirz enlisted in the Louisiana infantry and served in the Battle of Bull Run. His unit was assigned to Richmond, Virginia, and in the fall of 1861, Wirz became one of managers of the Richmond prison system. He earned a reputation as a hard master and callous leader. He excelled in the position and was promoted to sergeant in charge of ensuring the security of all military prisons in the city.

His next assignment was in Tuscaloosa, Alabama, where he was the assistant to Captain Elias Griswold. His first job was to move prisoners to an old hotel and provide security for the area. He was remembered there as a difficult manager of the men. One prisoner wrote in his diary, "We have Sergeant Wirz over us as a big tyrant as ever was."

Henry Wirz. *World Publishing Company.*

Wirz was soon promoted as head of the prison. One prison inmate described him as "a good fellow at times, and an unbelievably bad one at others. He would show his angular smile of half-stubborn good humor today and curse us in his fragmented English tomorrow."

He was next assigned to head the small camp in Andersonville, Camp Sumter. The camp was originally a prison facility. Construction of the new camp began in 1864, after the decision had been made to relocate Union prisoners from overcrowded prisons in Richmond to a more secure location. The idea was that the surrounding farms could easily provide enough beef, poultry, and vegetables to feed the prisoners.

Wirz was instructed to build a facility to house ten thousand prisoners. The stockade was constructed in the shape of a parallelogram that was 1,620 feet long and 779 feet wide, about the size of five football fields. At first, the site covered 16 acres but was expanded to cover 26 acres when the prison's population increased. It was enclosed by a 15-foot-tall stockade wall. Inside the wall, a low rail fence, about 20 feet inside the stockade wall called the "deadline." It was ensured that if a prisoner crossed it, a sniper was ready to shoot and kill him. Southern army guards were placed in towers called "Pigeon Roosts" 30 yards apart.

In late February 1864, the first prisoners arrived in Camp Sumter. The first group of four hundred inmates surprised Wirz; he was even more surprised that over the next few months, more than four hundred began arriving daily. He was quickly overwhelmed with the responsibility of providing housing, food, clothing, and medical care for such a large group of prisoners. There were only a few outhouses to provide showers and sanitary facilities for the prisoners. There was a small stream that ran

The execution of Henry Wirz. *World Publishing Company.*

through the camp, the Stockade Branch, a tributary of Sweetwater Creek; it should have provided drinking water, but the inmates used the stream to take care of their bodily needs instead.

As even more prisoners arrived, Wirz discovered he did not have enough supplies from the government to administer the camp. To make conditions worse, General Sherman was marching through Georgia on his drive to capture Atlanta. All the South's supplies were being used to provide for both armies. Wirz scoured the countryside, asking those surrounding the area to help supply the camp.

By the end of June, twenty-six thousand men were penned inside the camp. General John Winder arrived at the camp and worked to remedy the situation, but unfortunately, he died of a heart attack, leaving Wirz back in charge. By August, over thirty-three thousand inmates were held inside. Conditions in the camp became severe, as one Michigan cavalryman, John Ransom, wrote in his diary, "There is so much filth about the camp that it is terrible trying to live here. With sunken eyes, blackened countenances from pitch pine smoke, rags, and disease the men look sickening. The air reeks with nastiness."

Men started dying due to overcrowding, exposure, and the prison's poor sanitation, which brought on disease. Most died due to starvation. Inmates became skeletons, and the lack of clear, disease-free water added to their misery. Records found at the camp showed that, on average, ninety-six prisoners died each day.

Wirz buried the men side by side in trenches six-feet wide and four-feet deep. He did the best he could but was unable to come to any other solution to keep the other men safe.

To add to the horrific scene, fellow inmates called "raiders" formed squads to steal provisions from other prisoners. They terrorized and committed violence, including murder, against their fellow inmates. One group of raider leaders was captured, and, in a trial, found guilty and hanged.

Finally, after the capture of much of Georgia by General Sherman, Union prisoners at the camp were freed and sent to Union facilities back north. Camp Sumter's Andersonville Prison was closed for good. Out of the thirty thousand prisoners who were held in the camp, more than thirteen thousand died.

At the end of the war, newspapers across the country told stories of the horrors inflicted on the prisoners and the deaths of Northern inmates at Camp Sumter. The public demanded justice, and Captain Henry Wirz was arrested for his actions. In the trial that followed, he was accused of violating the rules of war. His defense attorney hoped to show that Wirz was just following orders from his superiors. But in October 1865, a military tribunal convicted him of war crimes, and Wirz was sentenced to be hanged. On November 10, 1865, a black hood was placed over his head, and he was brought to the place of his execution. His last words to the major in charge were: "I know what orders are, Major. And I am being hanged for obeying them."

Wirz was buried in Mount Olivet Cemetery in Washington, D.C.

After the trial, the famous poet Walt Whitman wrote, "There are deeds, crimes that may be forgiven but this is not among them. It steeps its perpetrators in blackest, escapeless, endless damnation."

Southerners were horrified at what happened to Wirz and felt that the general in charge of his unit was responsible. The idea that he was a scapegoat has continued through the ages.

In 1998, the National Prisoner of War Museum was opened in Andersonville. It is the only museum in the world that tells of the experiences of those who have been prisoners of war. The museum is dedicated to all those in America's past who have served their country with dignity and distinction so that current and future generations will be inspired by their service and sacrifice.

7

CENTRAL STATE HOSPITAL FOR THE INSANE

Georgia's Notorious Asylum and the Shame of Georgia Leaders Who Did Nothing to Help

In 1948, Dr. T.G. Peacock was appointed as acting superintendent of the Central State Hospital, a psychiatric institution dedicated to mental healthcare in the state of Georgia. Central State Hospital had been established in 1842 and was designed to care for those with mental illnesses and developmental disabilities. By the 1940s, it had grown to be the largest mental hospital in the United States. It housed more than twelve thousand patients and had more than two hundred buildings on two thousand acres of property.

Dr. Peacock was surprised by what he found at the hospital: The State of Georgia had created a hospital of horrors.

The trouble started when Georgia's state legislature created a new position: deputy welfare director for the hospital. The director thought he had been hired to oversee the hospital's operations and medical staff. Dr. Peacock had been hired as head of the hospital, so there was a conflict of authority between the new administrator and the physician.

Dr. Peacock led a revolt among the physicians, who all resigned. When all other outside doctors refused to fill the vacancies, the welfare director resigned. This episode caused a bitter divide between the hospital staff and the state legislature, and a committee was formed to resolve the crisis.

The committee visited the hospital and found surprising conditions at the institution. With Dr. Peacock leading the way, the committee found patients were forced to sleep on the floor and no showers were available.

Central State Hospital's main building, circa 1937. *Library of Congress.*

Half of the 9,500 patients were housed in unsafe, rundown buildings. The average stay of a patient at the hospital was twenty years, twice the amount expected at other institutions in the country. The committee found that attendants and nurses were having to work sixty to seventy hours per week, and most worked for as little as seventy dollars a month. Hospital physicians complained of the tremendous hours that were required to look after their patients. One doctor had 1,400 patients.

It was clear that the hospital's operations were being affected by the high turnover rate in medical staff. The committee found that most newly hired staff resigned only a few months after accepting their jobs. Another complaint was the constant pressure from outside political appointees to hire unqualified employees to run day-to-day operations.

The committee found that most of the hospital's treatment consisted entirely of shock therapy. More than three thousand patients had been given electric shock treatments. Many staff members believed that the treatments only were successful for a brief period, but most psychotic episodes would continue to recur.

The shock treatment at the hospital had many problems. The program was done on a mass assembly line, and many patients were forced to get on the shock table. After being shocked, they did not receive post-treatment care. They were confused and herded back to their rooms without any

The graves of asylum patients. *G. Miller.*

follow-up from staff. In addition, the committee found that many hospital patients had died without police or any other city or county officials being notified.

The report from the committee reads:

> *A male escaped from the hospital. A few days later his body was found on the riverbank a short distance from the hospital.*
>
> *The body of a male patient was found in the swamp near the hospital.*
>
> *A patient committed suicide by hanging himself with a sheet tied to the window of his room.*
>
> *One male patient died as a result of a severe beating about his face and head by another patient.*
>
> *On October 7, 1950, the body of a white man was found in the river near the hospital which was later identified as that of one of the patients.*

In one incident of brutality recorded by the committee, "a male patient confined to the Maximum-Security Building, died because of a handkerchief being stuffed in his throat. The male became ill and had to wipe up his vomit. Two attendants forced him to pick up his handkerchief and placed it back into his mouth, and in this process, he choked and died."

This instance was reported to authorities, and a grand jury indicted the attendants. But the jury was lenient and found them guilty of only a misdemeanor. Now, hospital staff had permission to use brutal treatment without fear of being punished for murder, as their harsh treatment would be classed as a misdemeanor.

Committee members found that the hospital used a radically different treatment for chronic patients. The treatment, a lobotomy, consists of severing the fibers that connect the frontal lobe with the rest of the brain. While some progress was achieved for a small group of patients, the treatment and results for an unknown number of patients were never reported. Today, lobotomies are considered a disparaged procedure, a byword for medical barbarism.

When results of the investigation were published, the public was outraged. After the committee sent the report to the governor and legislators, several laws were passed that helped the hospital deal with many of its issues. When the investigation of the hospital was completed, Dr. Peacock's changes were implemented.

His recommendations were:

1. The administration of the hospital should be under the state department of mental health, completely removed from partisan politics.
2. The admission of patients should be made by two physicians.
3. Patients should not wait in jail while for a commitment hearing.
4. The nonpsychotic patient (meaning those with a cognitive disability) should be placed in a special school.
5. Nonpsychotic alcoholics, drug addicts, and epileptics should be admitted.
6. Female staff should be paid the same as male staff in similar hospital positions.
7. More attendants are needed to staff the hospital.
8. Studies are needed to decide the effect of shock treatment on patients.
9. Toilet and bath facilities need to be upgraded.

Dr. Peacock also recommended that the legislature approve an expenditure of $6 million to address the problems listed in the report and $425,000 to upgrade employee housing.

In 1950 and 1952, many of the recommendations of the committee were placed into law, and conditions at the hospital improved. When Dr. Peacock left the hospital to pursue other interests, he had to know his influence on the improvement of Central Hospital was a great achievement.

In 1959, *Atlanta Journal-Constitution* reporter Jack Nelson reported more abuses at the hospital. His articles revealed that some physicians were drunk on duty, and one time, an unqualified nurse performed major surgery without a doctor's supervision. One damning story disclosed that the hospital gave experimental drugs to patients without family consent. Nelson won the Pulitzer Prize for his stories.

In 1963, President John F. Kennedy's Community Mental Health Act played a crucial role in changing the way mentally ill patients are treated and spurred the process of closing U.S. psychiatric hospitals known as deinstitutionalization. The law shifted focus to community-based mental healthcare, aiming to reduce the number of patients in state asylums. Local psychiatric care shifted to outpatient clinics, emergency services, and partial hospitalization. By 2013, the State of Georgia announced that most of Central State Hospital and Asylum had been closed for good.

Today, the mentally ill are often placed in jail or end up in camps for the unhoused. In Cobb County, a commission attempts to deal with more than 3,000 unhoused people who live in tents and get their food from churches and other nonprofit organizations. One survey stated that there are more than 2,500 unhoused children in Georgia's schools. There is a crisis of people experiencing homelessness all over the United States, and many who live in unhoused encampments are classified as mentally ill. There is an effort to produce solutions for Cobb County, and leaders want the solutions to come with compassion and understanding that all people should be treated with dignity. One official was quoted as saying, "There is no one single answer, but we have to try something."

8

DODGE LAND WARS

William E. Dodge, Carpetbagger: Murder and Mayhem for Fifty Years

In 1864, General William Sherman led the infamous March to the Sea that left Georgians devastated, with no money, their farm property unable to produce crops, and no timber products to sell.

After the war, many Northerners migrated to the state because they had the funds to take advantage of the local population. They were called "carpetbaggers" because they carried their clothes, money, and other items stuffed in carpetbags.

The worst carpetbagger in history was William E. Dodge, who led a group of other Northerners to steal three hundred thousand tracts of Georgia land using fake, questionable deeds. The property was set near Eastman in Southeast Georgia. The land held a large tract of longleaf pines—the most valuable crop in the state—equivalent to the size of Rhode Island. Citizens of this five-county region were descendants of the land's original settlers and believed they owned the rights to the land. Dodge's action started a fifty-year land war, which led to murder and mayhem over property rights between the locals and Dodge's carpetbaggers.

In 1886, Dodge hired lawyers and banking agents, who printed thousands of handbills and distributed them throughout the five counties claiming that Dodge had true title to the property. To confuse things, after the Civil War, someone named Dodge had sold much of the same land to hundreds of new citizens who had moved to the area and developed homesteads.

The Dodge Land Company moved to Eastman and Dublin and started brutally cutting down the longleaf pines. Many of the trees had grown in the area for hundreds of years. Millions of trees and more than three hundred

Honorable William E. Dodge.
Neely Young, Georgia Trend.

thousand acres were devastated. After the trees were removed, they were shipped on barges down the Altamaha River to the coast near Brunswick. There, they were milled and shipped to American, English, and European destinations. The locals fought Dodge through the courts and with guns and knives because they believed the land was theirs. But Dodge was wealthy enough to have New York lawyers, along with other resources, claim the land.

Eight men who opposed the land grab decided to do something desperate to stop the damage to their land. In 1890, they wanted to scare the Dodge agent, John C. Forsyth, who lived in Normandale, near McRae. Some of the men decided to kill him. To carry out their conspiracy, they hired a man named Rich Lowery. Lowery came from a backwoods town called Shuffletown, North Carolina. He was a notorious criminal and agreed to help the group murder Forsyth.

One evening in October, Forsyth was having dinner with his wife and child when, after desert, he took to his easy chair to light up a good cigar. Lowery appeared at the front door with a shotgun, pulled the trigger, and killed Forsyth. Then he ran into the woods to escape from the scene of the crime. According to records at the trial, Forsyth's child, Ellie, ran to her father's side to comfort him just before he died.

Several months later, the murder was still unsolved. But soon, a relative of one of the men involved was at a party and unwittingly told the group about the plot. Lowery could not be found, but the eight men who were part of the conspiracy were arrested. During the murder trial, Forsyth's young daughter, Nellie, gave the most convincing testimony, and the jury was sad to see the girl fatherless. Of the eight men, all but one was found guilty as charged and sentenced to long prison terms. The killer, Lowery, escaped. Rumors say he was murdered by one of Dodge's men and his body left in the swamp.

The land suit by local citizens went on for many years. The litigation for the thousands of landholders covered many pages, and the courts tried to determine who really owned the land. By 1923, many of the lawyers, judges, Dodge's attorneys, and the local citizens involved in the civil suit had died. The almost fifty-year dispute was finally settled in favor of the local citizens. The residents' land and property were finally made secure.

Dodge homestead. *Neely Young, Georgia Trend.*

Relatives of Dodge asked the state to name the area Dodge County for William E. Dodge. Yet most of the locals consider him a carpetbagger who made a fortune and took advantage of people during Reconstruction.

Later, Dodge's son, Anson Phelps Dodge Sr., took over the Dodge family sawmill in Brunswick. Anson's son, Anson Phelps Dodge Jr., became an Episcopalian priest and led Christ Church on St. Simons Island. The church had been destroyed by Yankee troops during General Sherman's march in 1864. It had been established in the early 1700s by Reverend John Wesley, who preached a sermon near a tree on St. Simons, so Anson rebuilt the new church right where Wesley had once stood. The site is now known as Wesley Oak and can be visited today. Anson established a trust fund to take care of the land around Christ Church.

The cemetery around the church holds the grave of John C. Forsyth and that of his daughter, Nellie. Unlike his hated grandfather, Reverend Anson Dodge died much beloved in 1898. You can visit his grave along with those of his wives, Ellen (1862–1883) and Anna (1927). Many of his children, grandchildren, and others live in the community today. The church is still in operation and is a testament to both the past and future of the little Island of St. Simons.

9

DOC HOLLIDAY

The Legend of the Swimming Incident in Valdosta

Joe Bradwell, editor of the *Valdosta Daily Times*, likes to tell stories of Doc Holliday, who was involved in the most famous gunfight of the American West. A Georgia native, Doc Holliday was a drinking buddy and gambling partner of Wyatt Earp, both heroes of the gunfight at the O.K. Corral, which was held in Tombstone, Arizona Territory, on October 26, 1881. The event was reproduced in a movie in 1957; Holliday's part is played by Kirk Douglas, and Earp is played by Burt Lancaster.

Bradwell's stories about young John Henry "Doc" Holliday's life in Valdosta are almost as big as the Tombstone event. Holliday was born in Griffin and spent the first twelve years of his life in Valdosta. His father, Major Henry Holliday, was a wealthy planter and druggist in Griffin who moved to Valdosta in early 1864, leaving Griffin to find a haven from the looming federal siege of Atlanta. After the war, Doc's father and family became prosperous citizens in the Valdosta community and purchased a home there that is still standing today. Major Henry was mayor of the city for sixteen years. John Henry was educated in Valdosta and graduated from dental school, thus gaining the nickname "Doc." But he had a wild, unpredictable temper and hated Yankees.

During post–Civil War Reconstruction, Union troops instituted martial law in Valdosta and established their headquarters at the Lowndes County Courthouse. A group of Union officers, along with the help of some outside Yankees—carpetbaggers—ran the city of Valdosta.

Some of the locals, including young Doc, decided to blow up the courthouse. The evening before a Yankee politician was scheduled to speak at the courthouse, locals broke in and planted dynamite in the basement. The plan was to light a long fuse, and just as the speaker was to begin, an explosion would rain down and kill the hated Union carpetbaggers. The plot was foiled when the young men discovered that many of their parents would be attending the event. The kegs of power were removed before any damage was done. Several of the young men who were part of the movement left town, but Doc stayed, and no punishment was ever meted out.

Doc Holliday in Prescott, Arizona, circa 1879. *Neely Young, Georgia Trend.*

Their story was called the "Swimming Hole Incident." A group of federal officers were using a swimming hole that was normally used by white residents near the fork of the Withlacoochee and Little Rivers at the settlement of Troupville, near Valdosta. According to local lore, Doc came upon the scene and ordered the officers, some of whom were Black, out of the water. When they refused, Doc reached for his gun. One of the men in the water ran to the bank and retrieved his gun for protection. But Doc, who had his "blood up," shot and killed one of the Black federal officers.

At the Valdosta-Lowndes County History Museum there is a section devoted to Doc, which documents his days living in the area. In one of the sections is the story of the shooting at the swimming hole, and it provides two theories about why Doc left Valdosta and moved west in 1873. One theory says that Doc contracted tuberculosis; the other says he left because of the swimming hole altercation. The museum piece relates that some versions of the tale say Doc shot and killed three people, while others say he shot only over their heads. "If true, Doc may have left to avoid arrest," per museum records.

No matter the reason, Doc was on his way to becoming a famous gambler, fighter, and hero of the movie *Gunfight at the O.K. Corral.*

Author Olin Jackson's book *Georgia's Doc Holliday* investigates these and other stories about Doc's early days. The two stories relayed by Bradwell cannot be confirmed by historical evidence and must go into the "myth" category of history. But there is no doubt that after Doc left Georgia "under a cloud," he became a tough, gunfighting, gambling character who, along with his girlfriend, "Big Nose Kate," and Wyatt Earp, walked into history during the gunfight at the O.K. Corral.

Many of Major Holliday's descendants are still fine citizens of Valdosta today, and they are proud of their association with Doc, as evidenced by the prominent place he holds in the local history museum.

10

EUGENE TALMADGE

Georgia's Crooked Governor

During the 1940s, Eugene Talmadge was governor of Georgia for three terms. No one was more infamous than Louisiana Governor Huey Long, who ruled his state with an iron hand, but Talmadge was Georgia's answer to Huey Long.

Talmadge dominated politics and actively ran for the governor's office on a platform that promoted white supremacy and segregation against Black people. He was born in Forsyth and attended the University of Georgia, where he received his law degree. He set up his practice in Telfair County.

He was elected state agriculture commissioner in 1926. During his term, Talmadge developed a reputation for being a man who disregarded ethics and ruled his office in a corrupt manner. He was accused of stealing $300,000 with an order that raised the price of hogs. When the media exposed his crooked crime, he famously campaigned all over the state telling voters, "Sure, I stole it! But I stole it for you."

In 1932, Talmadge ran for governor on a platform of limited government, low taxes, and segregation of the races. Georgia had a county unit system, which gave power to rural communities. A small county had the same number of electoral votes as the largest, including Fulton, the county in which the city of Atlanta is located. Talmadge easily won the election because his popular base was centered in small communities, where he told people he was the "poor man's friend."

Talmadge was a colorful character and campaigned by visiting every county courthouse, where he drew large crowds. He wore red suspenders

Eugene Talmadge. *Neely Young, Georgia Trend.*

and a straw hat. He took on the "rich Atlanta elite and those lying Atlanta newspapers." The crowd loved his speeches and screamed, "Give them hell, Gene!"

As governor, he continued his crooked ways at a much higher level. His favorite control method was calling martial law against any agency that failed to agree with him. When the state treasurer refused his orders, he had the state police remove him from office. When the state Department of Transportation defied his order to build a highway in his hometown, he fired the board members and installed his own people.

Talmadge kept getting elected and became a virtual dictator. He ran in 1931, 1934, and 1940 on the same platform that included the separation of the races. Voters in rural communities kept him in office because they believed he was a friend to the common man.

When the University of Georgia's Dean Walter Cocking advocated allowing Black students to attend the college, Talmadge called the board of regents and demanded they fire Cocking. The regents refused because they were a separate agency protected from the governor's control. Talmadge restructured the board and installed his own people as replacements. The new board fired Cocking, but the others went against the governor's orders. The Southern Association of Colleges removed accreditation for all Georgia state universities at the end of 1941, making students' degrees worthless.

Because of this school controversy, Talmadge lost the next election to a moderate challenger named Ellis Arnall. But Talmadge ran again in 1946 and promised he would restore a closed white primary election that excluded Black people from the voting process. It was his fourth victory in which he won by using the county unit system.

It's said Talmadge called an official in one Georgia county and asked him, "How many people have voted for me?" The official was a Talmadge man and replied, "How many do you need, Gene?"

After Talmadge won the December 1946 election, he passed away. Incredibly, after his death, he still tried to control the election, as he insisted in his will that his young son, Herman, take his place. This caused the infamous "Three Governors Controversy," which made Georgia a laughingstock of the nation. No fewer than three men claimed the office of Georgia's governorship: Gene's son, Herman; the outgoing governor, Ellis Arnall; and the newly elected lieutenant governor, Melvin E. Thompson.

The Georgia legislature met to decide who would be the new governor. Herman Talmadge seized the office and changed the locks on the door. Arnall set up a satellite office down the hall. He eventually gave up his claim and supported Thompson.

There's still more to the story, however. An *Atlanta Journal-Constitution* reporter named George Goodwin uncovered voting fraud in Talmadge's home in Telfair County. Goodwin discovered that some voters had risen from their graves; thirty-four deceased citizens appeared at the polls and voted in alphabetical order, starting with A and stopping at K. Goodwin won the Pulitzer Prize for exposing Eugene Talmadge's efforts to change the election, even after his death.

In March 1947, the Georgia Supreme Court ruled that Lieutenant Governor Thompson was the newly elected governor.

11
THE IGBO LANDING

Choosing Death Over Enslavement

In 1803, seventy-five enslaved people walked from their captive ship into the cool waters by St. Simons Island in what was the largest mass suicide in the history of the slave trade in America.

Slavery was a part of life in Georgia from the 1700s until the 1860s, although the British outlawed the practice in 1833. One of the largest enslaved groups were the Igbo people, who came from the region of what is now Nigeria in southeastern Africa.

Slavery was already present in many African societies long before the arrival of Europeans. African kingdoms used enslaved workers for domestic purposes, farming, and other forms of labor. Many enslaved people were captured in tribal wars. Organized raids on small villages were common, and in these raids, individuals, including women and children, were seized. People were also enslaved as a punishment for crime or for their failure to pay debts.

West Africa was a major source of enslaved laborers. The Kingdom of Dahomey, now a part of Benin, was notorious for its participation in the slave trade. It had a strong military tradition and often raided neighboring communities to take enslaved people. The Kingdom of Benin, in modern Nigeria, had a long history of slavery and engaged in slave raids as early as 1500 BCE.

The global trade transporting enslaved people from Africa to America moved 12 million people between the sixteenth and nineteenth centuries. Researchers believe that some 1.3 million of these people were from the Igbo region.

Above: Igbo Landing Area, Glynn County. *Public domain.*

Left: Igbo Landing marker, St. Simons. *Plaque from the Georgia Historical Society.*

The passage from Africa to the American colonies was brutal. Hundreds of enslaved Africans were packed into ship holds to endure unsanitary conditions and a lack of food and water. The captives were chained at the ankles and tied together with ropes around their necks. Historians believe 25 percent of enslaved Africans died on the passage to the New World.

The Igbo Landing of 1803. *Donovan Nelson, artist.*

One notorious example of the brutal treatment of enslaved prisoners was the action of Captain Luke Collingwood. The prisoners on his ship, the *Zong*, were infected with disease, so Collingwood had 130 enslaved people thrown overboard. He filed an insurance claim with the Lord of England Insurance Company for the value of his enslaved prisoners. He claimed that his "cargo was no different than cattle being thrown overboard."

When Savannah and Fort Frederic Township were established in 1733, African slavery was outlawed in the new colony. The English Trustees of Georgia believed the institution to be against their ideals. The trustees also banned lawyers from being allowed into the new colony. But the enslaved people in other colonies could find their way to freedom by escaping through Georgia to the coast of Spanish Florida. There, if they converted to Catholicism and agreed to fight for the Spanish, they were set free.

In September 1739, enslaved people from South Carolina killed enslavers and seized weapons and ammunition. They wandered through Georgia to Florida to find freedom. Called the Stono Rebellion, it was the largest revolt of enslaved people in the mainland British colonies. Between sixty to one hundred enslaved Africans fought in the uprising, and about forty Black and twenty white people were killed.

Spain was at war with England and was a major threat to the British colonies in the New World. The War of Jenkins' Ear was a dispute between Spain and Great Britain that lasted from 1738 to 1748. It was settled in 1748, when the two countries signed a peace agreement. Because the British Crown was no longer worried about enslaved people escaping to Florida through Georgia, Parliament replaced the Act of 1735 with legislation that allowed slavery.

With the invention of the cotton gin in 1793, Georgia began importing enslaved laborers to harvest cotton. By the early 1800s, fourteen different plantations were operating on St. Simons alone. In 1803, Thomas Spalding and John Couper of St. Simons came to Savannah to buy seventy-five Igbo people for $100 each from a local slave market. The enslaved people had been taken from Nigeria and transported to Georgia on a ship called the *Wanderer*. The Igbo captives were then transported to a ship called the *York* and brought to St. Simons, an inland port about one hundred miles south of Savannah.

In 1793, Couper bought Cannon Point in northeast St. Simons. The plantation's main crop was cotton; it is still produced there today and is known as Sea Island Cotton. Couper also grew indigo, grapes, olive trees, sugar cane and other crops that used slave labor to harvest the crops.

As the *York* sailed to the island, near Dunbar Creek, the Igbos rebelled against the small crew and threw them overboard. Then the Igbos, who decided that dying was better than living in slavery, walked into the water of Dunbar Creek and drowned. History records that the Igbos chose mass suicide over existing as the property of other people. They were heard singing in their native language: "By the water spirits we came and by the water spirits we will be taken home. You cannot be an enemy of the land you are part of."

The story of the Igbo Landing was passed down through the oral tradition of enslaved people in America and their descendants. Legend says the captives flew or walked on water back to their home in Africa. In one oral account, called "The Myth of the Flying Africans," a man named Wallace Quarterman said that the Igbo people disliked their treatment and transformed themselves into buzzards to fly home. Other stories say their spirts were trapped in the water and that the Igbo Landing is haunted and sacred.

The Gullah descendants of the enslaved are still living on St. Simons and other islands in the area. One, Sapelo Island, is where Thomas Spalding's plantation was located. Today, the last of the Gullah people live in the Hog Hammock community and still pass on the traditional stories of their people. These citizens have developed an economy based on their arts and crafts. Sapelo Island has been under stress recently by developers who want to build condominiums and homes around the island. To date, the island's building codes have prevented this from happening.

Sapelo Island and Hog Hammock are living connections to West African languages, folk stories, and spiritual traditions, including the legend of the Igbo Landing.

12

GENERALS JUBAL EARLY AND JAMES LONGSTREET

An Epic Feud After the Civil War

When the Civil War ended in 1865, no man was more vilified and shamed by his own fellow Southerners than native Georgian and Confederate General James Longstreet. Another 110 years passed before he was vindicated by Michael Shaara's 1970 Pulitzer Prize–winning book, *The Killer Angels*. And there was no story more powerful than that of General Longstreet and his feud with General Jubal Early.

For the first few years of his life, Longstreet was raised on his father's farm outside Gainesville, Florida. When he was nine, following the death of his father, his family decided a military career was in James's future and sent him to live with his uncle in Augusta so he could be better educated at the Richmond County Academy. From that point on, he was raised by his uncle Augustus Baldwin Longstreet, who was almost as famous as the general. Augustus was a lawyer, judge, Methodist minister, educator, college president, newspaper editor, and author. He was Emory University's (then Emory College's) second president and was a nationally known humorist and author of the classic *Georgia Scenes*.

Through his uncle's influence, Longstreet received an appointment to West Point in 1838. During his college days, Longstreet's best friends were men who became Union generals, including Ulysses S. Grant, William Tecumseh Sherman, George Pickett, and William S. Rosecrans. After graduating from West Point, he fought alongside Pickett in the Mexican-American War.

Jubal Early was born in Franklin, Virginia, and was appointed as a cadet to West Point in 1833. He most likely crossed paths with Longstreet during

Jubal Early. *Longstreet Society Historic Piedmont Hotel and Museum.*

this time. After his graduation, Early was sent to Florida, where he fought in the Second Seminole War and later participated in the 1847 Mexican-American War.

On January 1, 1847, Early joined the Confederate army as a colonel in the Virginia Infantry. He was promoted to major general and distinguished himself in almost every major battle of the war, included Gettysburg, where he served under General James Longstreet. After the war, Early returned to his law practice, where he became a major advocate in the Lost Cause movement.

Longstreet enlisted in the Confederate army after the Battle of Fort Sumter and soon rose through the ranks to become one of General Robert E. Lee's best generals. His battle plan was typically to pick a higher ground position, dig in, and let the enemy charge uphill. The Yankees would soon wear themselves out. At that point, Longstreet would counterattack with powerfully destructive results. After many victories, including Fredericksburg, Longstreet was known by his soldiers as the "best fighter in the whole army."

Longstreet was never far from Lee, who called him his "Old War Horse," as he relied heavily on his judgment.

In a story published in *Harper's Weekly*, the top national newspaper of the time, Longstreet is described as "perhaps, since the death of Stonewall Jackson, second only to Lee in the military reputation he has achieved by the campaigns between Washington and Richmond during the last three years."

After many Union losses, a victory at the Battle of Gettysburg in July 1863 proved to be the turning point in the war for the federal troops and set them on their path to victory. In the South, debate has raged for 150 years over who was responsible for the loss at Gettysburg.

During the second day of battle, Early's troops were at the base of Culp's Hill, next to Cemetery Ridge, and should have taken the position. This would have given the Confederates the higher ground for the main battle the next day. But Union troops retained possession of East Cemetery Hill, and Early hesitated and then withdrew, an action that would have devastating results.

Two days later, Lee ordered one of Longstreet's divisions, led by General George Pickett, to charge Cemetery Hill. Lee felt that a Confederate victory at this position in enemy territory, near Washington, D.C., could end the war. Longstreet disagreed and wanted to move Confederate troops into a

James Longstreet. *The History Press. Longstreet Society Historic Piedmont Hotel and Museum.*

position that would put them on higher ground and on the defense so that Union troops would be under unfavorable conditions and forced to charge uphill to attack. He told Lee that his order to charge up Cemetery Hill would be disastrous.

When Lee ordered Longstreet to have Pickett charge the middle of the Union lines, Longstreet tried to resign. Lee refused his friend's resignation, and Pickett's Charge failed, resulting in a decisive Union victory that changed the course of the war. Lee retreated into Virginia, and the Confederacy never recovered, even though the war lasted another two years.

After the war, during Reconstruction, the South's devastation was intensified by Northern exploitation. President Abraham Lincoln had been a member of the liberal Republican Party, which was founded on the principle of freeing the enslaved. The South was solidly Democratic, conservative, and protective of slavery. Anyone who was a Republican was considered a traitor or "on the other side" by 98 percent of Southerners. A movement called the Lost Cause was formed, and people below the Mason-Dixon line came to believe the South's defeat was honorable. Those who supported the Yankees were called "scalawags."

Longstreet believed that his fellow Southerners should put the war behind them and accept Black Americans as equal citizens under the law. He did the unthinkable and joined the Republican Party. The governor of Louisiana appointed him the adjutant general of the state militia. Southerners were shocked when Longstreet used Black troops to put down a white rebellion in New Orleans.

Early was elected head of the Association of the Army of Northern Virginia, a veterans' group, in 1870 and wrote a long newspaper column expressing his view that Longstreet was a disgrace to the Lost Cause. As a consequence, Longstreet's family faced social ostracism. Then Early "pulled out the long knives." In a speech in Virginia, he accused Longstreet of being responsible for the loss at Gettysburg. He said Longstreet delayed the uphill charge, which gave the Union troops time to reinforce the center.

His words were false. Early's failure to take Culp's Hill the first day of the battle added to the failure of his commander, General Richard Ewell, who was slow to take the hill. It was Ewell's dalliance the day before, historians say, that was one of the main causes for the Confederate loss at Gettysburg.

This is a political trick that is still used today—attack your opponent's reputation in a manner that defies rebuttal. Lee had passed away by the time of Early's speech, but he must have been turning over in his grave to hear the false claim made against his best general.

For the next forty years, Longstreet was a Judas for many in the South. He and Early battled it out in newspaper columns and books on the subject. Many historians at the time believed Early, and some wrote histories blaming Longstreet for the loss at Gettysburg.

Longstreet retired to a farm near Gainesville and operated the large Piedmont Hotel. In 1896, he wrote his book, *From Manassas to Appomattox*, which added fuel to the fire by blaming Lee for the loss. His comments on page 405 state: "It does not look like generalship to lose a battle and a cause and then lay the responsibility upon others. If he [Lee] failed to apply the remedy, it was his fault." His book caused a firestorm of criticism from the Lost Cause crowd, and it was debated in the national press for many years after.

After many years of feuding between the men, Early died in Lynchburg, Virginia, in 1894. Longstreet died peacefully in 1904. He outlived all his fellow generals. It took more than one hundred years for the truth to come out and help restore Longstreet's reputation. Shaara's book *The Killer Angels* tells the real story of Gettysburg. Several years later, the movie *Gettysburg*, produced by another famous Georgian, Ted Turner, helped set the record straight.

Today, there is a Longstreet Society, based in Gainesville, that tracks the general's legacy. In 1998, the group led a successful effort to place a statue of Longstreet at the Gettysburg National Military Park, one of the last monuments erected in the park. It has also restored the remaining section of the Piedmont Hotel in Gainesville.

In the 1960s, another famous Georgian who shares the Longstreet name, the late Charles Longstreet Weltner, then a Georgia congressman and later chief justice of the Georgia Supreme Court, was an outspoken opponent of segregation. He made a national name for himself when he chose to give up his seat in Congress rather than sign a Democratic Party loyalty oath that required him to support segregationist Lester Maddox for governor.

As an aside, Pickett, who led the charge up Cemetery Ridge, never believed Early's accusation that Longstreet lost the Battle of Gettysburg. When asked why the South lost at Gettysburg, Pickett replied, "I think the Yankees had something to do with it."

13

JULIAN AND JULIA HARRIS

How Dishonest Sheriffs and Other Public Officials Failed to Protect a Local Journalist

Julian Harris was the son of Joel Chandler, the famous editor and essayist who wrote the Uncle Remus stories. In 1920, Harris and his wife, Julia, came to Columbus, Georgia, and purchased the *Columbus Enquirer-Sun*. The town, like many others in the Deep South, was still recovering from the effects of the Civil War and Reconstruction. The white political structure kept Black people in their designated place. Black families were housed in restricted areas. Black citizens had no rights—they were not even allowed to vote—and their children were placed in a separate school system with no options for advancement.

Across the South, the practice of lynching—the killing of a Black man through mob violence—was prevalent. If a Black man talked with a white woman in public, he could be arrested and jailed. The Ku Klux Klan was an active organization in the Deep South, if Black men weren't careful, they could be taken from prison and hanged. A Black man had no protection from the sheriff or other court officials.

Harris used his newspaper to crusade for social justice and took on the Klan, a secret organization whose members wore white hoods to hide their identities. In one issue, the *Enquirer-Sun* exposed Klan members by publishing their names.

Opposite: Julia Collier Harris. *Above*: Joel Chandler Harris. *Library of Congress.*

The Harrises put their lives at risk, and the Klan tried to stop their editorials by burning crosses in front of their home. After the cross-burning event, the newspaper kept on writing editorials which condemned the treatment of Black Georgians. In one editorial column, the Harrises demanded that racist, dishonest, and incompetent public officials, including the sheriff, resign their offices. The couple also wrote other stories condemning other laws, including one that barred the teaching of evolution in schools. The newspaper became famous, and the Harris influence spread to other Southern newspapers. Many other publishers took up the Harrises' cause.

In 1926, Julian and Julia Harris and the *Columbus Enquirer-Sun* were awarded the Pulitzer Prize. The award cited the couple for "their brave and energetic fight against the Ku Klux Klan; against the enactment of a law barring the teaching of evolution; against dishonest and failed public officials and for justice for Blacks and against lynching."

Despite this great honor, the newspaper fell on hard times. The Klan pressured advertisers to stop placing advertisements in the newspaper, and in 1929, the Harrises lost it. They moved from Columbus to Atlanta, and Julian became the Southern correspondent for the *New York Times*. Later, the Harrises were inducted into the Georgia Writers of Hall Fame, the state's highest honor for writers.

14

JOHN PRIOR

The Phillips Colquitt Gang: Violent Killers and How John Prior Brought Them to Justice

Author's note: The surname Prior was changed after the family moved from the Carolinas to Georgia in the nineteenth century.

After Lee and Grant's famous meeting at Appomattox, when the Civil War ended, a bloody fight took place in Cedartown. If you've heard stories from the Wild West, this clash resembled the gunfight at the O.K. Corral, yet it was held in Georgia.

As part of the sesquicentennial commemoration of Georgia's role in the "War Between the States," an article published in the *Rome News* in 1897 tells the story of the gun fight between John Prior and the Phillips Colquitt Gang in the small town south of Rome.

John's grandfather Asa Prior first came to Polk County in 1833, after the Cherokee Land Lottery. Asa's father, along with other families, founded the beautiful town of Cedartown. They were fine people who established a trading post and farm in the area. Fast-forward thirty-one years to 1864, and Prior and his son Haden were trying to recover from the devastation of their community being put to the torch by Kilpatrick's Yankee calvary, who were chasing Confederate General John Bell Hood's troops as they retreated while Sherman burned Atlanta.

As the war ended, outlaw raiders came in behind the Yankees robbing, looting, murdering, and maiming many of the harmless civilians who were left behind. There was no civil law, and these scalawags, as they were called, laid waste to the countryside. To counter this situation, Georgia Governor Joe

Left: John Prior. *Right*: Haden Prior. *Gordon D. Sargent.*

Brown organized a loose group of former soldiers called the Home Guard to help provide law and order in the state. Brown appointed Haden Prior to head the Cedartown command. At this time, an outlaw group headed by scalawag Phillips Colquitt was raiding local farms, and Haden appointed his son John to form a posse to track the gang down and bring them to justice.

John's group picked up the Colquitt Gang's trail near Cave Springs and closed in. When the raiders saw the Home Guard, they turned their horses and headed for the hills. John raised his gun and fired at the group, and one man fell dead off his horse. The others were caught but later escaped and were soon terrorizing the countryside again.

The Colquitt Gang plotted revenge. John's father, Haden, was visiting a friend near his home when the Colquitt Gang confronted him at the front gate. Colquitt drew his pistol and shot Old Man Prior through the heart, killing him instantly. After a sad funeral, John saddled up and wasted no time in hunting down the killers.

He found one of the gang members alone on the road and shot and killed him. Later, he found more of the gang and told the following story, as it was quoted in the Rome newspaper:

> *It was between 11 or 12 o'clock when just beyond Coloma, Alabama, I rode up in front of the Widow Lane's house and saw two men sitting under*

some trees and three horses tied nearby. The men, I think, saw me about the same time I saw them. One of them made a movement to reach for his gun. I jumped off my horse, cocked my double-barrel shotgun and fired before he raised his. One of them fell over riddled with buckshot, while the other ran around the house. I drew my pistol and ran after him, but just around the corner came upon his dead body where he fell.

A third man ran into the woods and thought he had escaped, but Prior caught up with him and shot him dead.

With the earlier killings, John Prior had tracked down and killed five men, three in less than twenty-four hours. But his father's killer, Phillips, was still at large. Prior discovered that he was hiding out in the West Georgia community of Haralson County, near the small settlement of Tallapoosa. John continued: "It was early July that I with one of my brothers and two friends started out about nightfall for Phillips's home with the determination of killing him. We surrounded his home sometimes about 3 o'clock in the morning."

Early in the morning, Phillips came out of his house and went out into a field to begin plowing and planting a crop. Prior went to the top of a nearby hill and dismounted his horse. He concealed himself in the undergrowth and waited until Phillips came close. Prior jumped out of the bushes and pulled his gun. "Phillips," he said, "I want you!"

According to the newspaper, Phillips begged to be able to go see his wife. Prior asked him to confess to killing his father, Haden, but the man denied doing so. About that time, Phillips's wife and children came out of their house and watched from a distance. Prior replied that he had evidence that Phillips had done the killing and that he was also the leader of the gang that was raiding, murdering, and terrorizing the citizens of Polk County. Phillips fell to the ground and begged for his life. Prior replied, "You needn't expect any mercy from me. I'm going to kill you."

Phillips broke into a run across the field toward his house. When he did this, Prior shot him. Phillips fell on his side and rolled over onto his back. Next, Prior walked over, pointed his pistol at Phillips's heart, and pulled the trigger at close range. It was over. After this killing spree, the rest of the Colquitt Gang left Cedartown and headed west. Polk County became a peaceful community again.

Prior had killed six men and was considered a hero by everyone in Polk County. He was never charged with murder or any other crime because people wanted to honor him—they didn't want prosecute someone who had risked his life to protect their lives and property. Prior lived a quiet, peaceful life and finally passed away in 1910 at the ripe old age of seventy. He and his children had moved west, so there are few Prior descendants left in Cedartown today.

The events described in this chapter show that the Wild West we read about in the history books was actually the Wild West of West Georgia. The same murders and horrendous events described here were commonplace all over the South right after the war ended. The old mill associated with the Asa Prior family is still standing in Cedartown, and Little Cedar Creek rushes over the old mill's dam. Like the waters of time, this creek bears memory of a small piece of violent history now gone with the wind.

15
THE MACHETTI MURDERS

Rebecca Machetti, a Woman Whose Level of Wickedness Spared No One, Not Even Her Own Daughters

Rebecca "Becky" was born in 1938 in Athens to Coy and Sara Turpin. She lived as an only child until she was fourteen. In 1952, the Turpins became parents of a new baby named Michael.

Coy was a fine father to his children and had no history of abusing alcohol or any drugs. He loved his son and played with him each evening when he came home from work.

The family had a housekeeper named Janie Goolsby. Coy came home from work early one day November in 1955. He took Michael to the bathroom and closed the door. Goosby was working in the kitchen and thought they were staying in the bathroom longer than normal. She knocked on the door, and when no one answered she entered the room. She found the child on the floor covered in blood and Coy lying beside him. Both had been killed by a shotgun.

The police decided the deaths were the result of a murder/suicide. The coroner chose not to order an inquest because he thought Turpin had killed himself and his son. They blamed the crime on the father, saying he'd had a mental breakdown. The Turpins' daughter, Becky, was enrolled in a school near the home. There was no reason to investigate further.

In 1955, Becky married Ronny Akins and moved to Macon. Over the next few years, they had three daughters: Victoria Ramona, Valerie Rhonda, and Vanessa Rebecca. Over the years, Becky became difficult and hard to deal with. Her behavior was erratic, and she became hysterical when things did not go her way. Without her husband's knowledge, she started seeing other

The Machetti murders. *Online Athens.*

men on the side. She would take the girls to a park and then leave them to go meet other men.

The three girls grew to be teenagers, and Ronny tried to keep their family together, even under difficult circumstances. At supper one night in August 1973, Becky served Ronny a milkshake. He thought it tasted funny and soon came down with a headache. The girls had seen their mother put paint remover into the drink. He stumbled into their bedroom. They heard their father throwing up and moaning. They ran into the room and found their mother lying across him. The girls were directed to hold down Ronny's legs while Becky grabbed a pillow and started pressing it on his face. Soon, Ronny became still. The next morning, the girls went to school and Becky drove off to town, as if nothing had happened.

When Ronny did not show up for work, his boss drove to his house, where he found Ronny's body lying on the floor. He was still breathing, and an ambulance was called to take him to the hospital. He survived and told authorities, "My wife tried to kill me."

The couple divorced, and Becky took her three teenage daughters and moved to Miami, Florida. On June 1, 1974, she met John Eldon Smith. Smith confided in her that he wanted to join the mafia, and she convinced him he should change his name to one that sounded more Italian. He changed his name to Anthony Machetti, and soon after, Becky became Mrs. Anthony Machetti. Later, she met another man, John Maree Jr., who was connected to the Miami mafia. The three became fast friends, and Anthony asked John how he could become a hit man for the mob.

Becky concocted a scene in which her new husband could impress the mafia—by killing her previous husband. She offered Maree $1,000 to drive Machetti to Macon to carry out the crime. She threatened to shoot Maree if he did not go along with her plan. To pay for the crime, Becky planned to cash in an insurance policy she had received as part of her divorce from Ronny Akins. Next, she obtained from a doctor a poisonous drug that she planned to use in the murder.

Becky gave the two men a map to guide them to Macon and her ex-husband's home. They were to knock him out and administer the poison.

But when they drove to Akins's home, they found he wasn't there. Akins had recently married Juanita Knight on August 11, 1974. The two men found the couple and convinced Akins and his new wife to go to a wooded area. The Akinses believed Machetti was going to install a TV antenna for them.

According to testimony given at the trial, Maree said: "When the Akins arrived, Machetti pulled a pistol and ordered the couple out of the car and had them place their hands on the roof of the car. Machetti tried to knock Akins out by hitting him on the back of his head with the pistol. Akins fought back, and Machetti went to his car and came back with a shotgun. Mrs. Akins started screaming and ran to the car to call for help on their two-way radio....There were three shots. I am not sure who was shot first."

Machetti and Maree then drove back to Miami, stopping only to call Becky to report that they had bagged "a big fish."

When they returned to Becky's house in Miami, Maree said "she was pleased everything went well."

The Akinses' bodies were discovered by Quinton Cotton, a Pan American pilot who was flying overhead in a private plane on a pleasure trip. As he was flying over the area near Wesleyan College, he and his fiancée spotted a white Mustang and saw Akins lying on the ground near his car. Cotton notified the Bibb County sheriff, and deputies found the Akinses bodies soon after. Investigators found a palm print on the car, and an expert from the Atlanta Crime Laboratory identified it as John Maree's. The Miami police were contacted, and they found and arrested Maree. Maree told officials what had happened, and he and the Machettis were arrested and placed into custody.

The three were transferred from Miami to Macon. In Bibb County Superior Court in separate jury trials, all three were convicted of the murders of John and Juanita Akins.

In John Smith's (alias Anthony Machetti) trial, the jury took only twenty minutes to reach a verdict. He was sentenced to death. According to Georgia law, the appeal of a death sentence is automatic. A stay of execution was denied, and on December 15, 1983, John Eldon Smith was executed by the state of Georgia via the electric chair at the age of fifty-three.

John Maree Jr. pleaded guilty to the 1974 slaying. He was offered a reduced sentence, and prosecutors promised they would not seek the death penalty in return for his testimony against the Machettis. He received two life sentences. He was later paroled, and at the time of Machetti's death, he was living in North Carolina.

Rebecca "Becky" Machetti, thirty-nine, was sentenced to die in the electric chair, the only woman in Georgia's history to face the death penalty. At the time, she was joined by only four other women on death row in the United States.

She waited four years in prison before her case was overturned on appeal. Her conviction was overturned when the Eleventh U.S. Circuit Court of Appeals ruled there had been too few women on the grand and trial juries that indicted and convicted her.

On July 28, 1983, Becky's second trial was moved to Gwinnett County, where a jury found her guilty of murdering the Akinses. In the trial, her daughter told of the horror that occurred when Becky told the girls to hold down their father's legs as she tried to kill him. But her death sentence was reduced to life in prison. The jury held that since Becky had no earlier criminal record and was not at the scene of the crime at the time of the Akinses' deaths, she should be spared the death penalty.

In 1984, Becky applied for parole but was denied by the state board of pardons and parole. She was not eligible for parole review for the next three years, the longest interval allowed by board policy considerations. She continued to apply for parole every three years for thirty-six years but was always denied. She was finally released for good behavior in 2010. Rebecca "Becky" Turpin Akins Machetti died in September 2020 from complications of COVID-19. She was eighty-one. In her first trial, she was correctly described as: "A woman whose level of wickedness spared no one, not even her own daughters."

16

MOORE'S FORD LYNCHING

Barrnett Hester, John Harrison, and the 1945 Moore's Ford Killing

George W. Dorsey was a Black veteran of World War II who was back in the United States after serving five years in the Pacific theater. George and May Dorsey and Dorothy Malcom, the wife of Roger Malcom, were driving with a white man named J. Loy Harrison, who was taking them to post a $600 bail for Malcom. He was in jail for allegedly stabbing a white man. But the two Black couples had no idea what was waiting for them on a road between Monroe and Watkinsville.

In 1946, three-time governor Eugene Talmadge was trying to get reelected and was in a political fight with a moderate candidate, James V. Carmichael. In what was a typical dirty trick, Talmadge pulled out the race card and tried to paint Carmichael as a man who loved Black people. During his earlier term, Talmadge controlled politics in the state. He was a strong man and political figure and did as he pleased without any care for the rule of law. For example, he was accused of stealing $100,000 in state funds. Instead of fighting the charge, Talmadge confessed to the crime. He went to political rallies all over the state to tell people: "Yes, I stole, but I stole for you, the people of Georgia."

At the end of the campaign, Talmadge boasted that he flogged the Black sharecroppers who worked on his farm. He told other stories of violence with racist rhetoric intent on abusing Black people. He was proud of the time he'd taken an axe and chased a Black man who dared to walk on the street with a white woman. When *Atlanta Journal-Constitution* columnist Ralph

Moore's Ford lynching. *Plaque from the Georgia Historical Society.*

McGill wrote an editorial that reported Talmadge was a member of the Ku Klux Klan, the governor proudly admitted to the claim.

At a rally in Monroe, Talmadge talked with two local farmers, Barnette Hester and J. Loy Harrison, both longtime supporters. Harrison had even named one of his sons after Talmadge. According to an FBI report released in 2007, Talmadge offered immunity to anyone "'taking care' of a Negro."

Harrison was driving the three couples back to his farm when he stopped his car near the Moore's Ford Bridge. There, fifteen to twenty armed white men were waiting for them. According to a statement made after the event, Harrison said:

> *A big man who was dressed proud in a double-breasted brown suit was giving the orders. He pointed to Roger Malcom and said, "We want that* [Black man]*." Then he pointed to George Dorsey and said, "We want you, too, Charlie."*
>
> *Harrison said, "His name is George."*
>
> *"Keep your damned big mouth shut. This ain't your party."*
>
> *One of the women knew one of the assailants. The man ordered to get those women, too.*

The mob took the couples to a big oak tree and tied them up. The white men fired some sixty shots at close range at the couples. They killed the two couples on a dirt road near Moore's Ford Bridge. After the crime, the assailants quietly disappeared. Harrison left the scene and reported the event to local police. He claimed he did not know who the men were.

The murders caused national outrage and were covered by newspapers and radio stations all over the country. In Washington, D.C., President Harry Truman directed the FBI to offer a $12,500 award to "anyone for giving any information that would help arrest and convict persons involved in the killing of four Negroes in Walton County on July 25, 1946." He also created the President's Committee on Civil Rights, which introduced an antilynching bill to Congress. Georgia Governor Ellis Arnall offered a reward of $10,000 for information that would help solve the crime.

Local law enforcement, the Georgia Bureau of Investigation, and the FBI worked for more than four months to find the mob involved in the lynching. The FBI interviewed more than three thousand people but could not find any evidence to indict anyone. They determined that the residents of Walton County were reluctant to give out information because they resented outsiders coming to their city. Black people in the area were afraid and evaded questioning about the lynching, as they felt they might be lynched themselves.

Harrison continued to claim he did not know any of the people involved. The FBI and police suspected he might have been involved in making plans to carry out the crime. None of the mob wore masks, and his claim he did not know any of them was widely disbelieved. One police official said, "Harrison is either scared of being killed himself or he's lying through his teeth or both."

Walter Clark, the director of the National Association for the Advancement of Colored People, wrote to President Truman that the Moore's Ford Lynching was "the direct result of a conspiratorial campaign to violate the U.S. Constitution by Eugene Talmadge and the Ku Klux Klan."

At the end of the investigations, no evidence was found, and no one was brought to trial.

A funeral was held for the Dorsey and the Malcom families at the local Mount Perry Church. George Dorsey was a World War II veteran, so an American flag was placed on his coffin. Many Black residents attended the funeral, but many others stayed away because they were afraid. A journalist from the Black-owned newspaper the *Chicago Defender* reported that one Black man said, "They are trying to exterminate us. They are killing Negro veterans, and we do not have anything to fight back except our bare hands."

On December 2, 1946, a federal grand jury investigation heard testimony in the case. For three weeks, many people testified before the jury, included Harrison, his sons, a group of farmers who lived near the location of the killings, and others. On the seventh day of testimony, six Black people were questioned, but none could give any up-to-date information. The wife of a local minister testified that she had seen men gather on a roadside in the vicinity of Monroe between the jail and the site of the incident at Moore's Ford. The jury considered her testimony, but after three weeks of hearings, the grand jury found no new evidence. They were "unable to establish the identity of any persons guilty of violating the civil rights statute of the United States."

In 1945, Eugene Talmadge won the governor's election but died before he took office. He was never investigated for his part in the lynching at Moore's Ford.

In 1999, the Georgia Historical Society placed a historical marker near the murder site. It was erected on the fiftieth anniversary of the last unsolved mass lynching in America. During the ceremony, there was a military memorial service to honor George Dorsey, the murdered World II veteran.

In January 2018, the Georgia Bureau of Investigation officially closed any effort to bring perpetrators of the lynching to justice. Despite major investigations from police, the GBI, and the FBI, no culprits were ever found or prosecuted for the slaying of the two families.

17
MURDER IN COWETA COUNTY

John Wallace: The Meanest Man in Georgia

John Wallace was a wealthy farmer and cow calf operator in Meriwether County, near Warm Springs. The area is famous for the Little White House, which was used by President Franklin Roosevelt during his visits to the area.

Wallace owned a two-thousand-acre farm, which he named the Kingdom, and he considered himself the "King" of the entire county. People in the community put up with his arrogant, overbearing manner because he was good at contributing to his church and other causes in town.

Wallace had many Black tenants on his property. To them, he was a vicious man, and his racist attitude showed no positive feeling for those who worked on his farm.

In 1948, many descendants of the formerly enslaved still lived on the farms owned by their enslavers. When the enslaved were freed after the war, they had no education or any way to a make a living other than remaining to farm in the same place. Many Southern states enacted laws that denied Black citizens their equal rights. Black citizens could not vote or own property and were placed in communities that were "red lined" to separate them from white residents. The "separate but equal" laws kept Black and white citizens separated in schools, public restaurants, and other facilities. In some states, a Black man could not talk to or be in the company of a white woman without being arrested. And in courthouses and other public facilities, there were separate bathrooms and water fountains for white and Black people.

Many Black people were a part of the sharecropper system, which allowed a tenant to farm the land owned by another. The landowner would

Murder in Coweta County. Margaret Anne Barnes.

provide a home for these farmers and would them money to buy the seed and equipment necessary to manage a crop. At harvest time, the crop would be sent to market. The landowner would take their cut of the profit and take out expenses, including interest on the loan, rent on the sharecroppers' homes, and other expenses. Then the sharecroppers would receive their small share of what was left. Many times, there would no profit left for the Black or white workers.

In April 1948, Willam Turner was a Black sharecropper who worked the land for John Wallace. Turner also did odd jobs for Wallace. Turner and Wallace got into a dispute over payment Turner said he was owed. Wallace fired Turner and kicked him and his family off his property.

But Turner wanted to receive his payment, so one night he stole one of Wallace's prized Guernsey cows. Wallace found the cow and had Turner arrested. While Turner had pastured the cow in a field in Carroll County, Wallace had a lot of influence in his home county of Meriwether and arranged for Turner to be transferred to a jail there. Wallace conspired with Meriwether County Sheriff Hardy Collier for Turner's release from the jail. Turner left the jail and got into his pickup truck to go home. But Wallace and his compatriots were waiting for him. When Turner left in his truck, Wallace and a driver named Herring Sivell took off in hot pursuit, followed by Henry Mobley and Tom Strickland in another car.

Turner was chased up Highway 27 to Coweta County, just across the Meriwether County line. Turner's car seemed to run out of gas, and the frightened cattle rustler swerved into the parking lot of the Sunset Motel and Tourist Camp. Wallace grabbed Turner out of his truck and hit him in the back of his head with the barrel of a shotgun. Wallace killed the man in cold blood. He put Turner in his car and beat a hasty retreat to his home in Meriwether County. Wallace then put Turner's body in a well before he later retrieved and burned it. Then he buried the remains in the woods near his house, where he thought no one could find them.

After the murder, Wallace had taken Turner's body across the county line between Coweta and Meriwether Counties. The murder was carried out in

Coweta County, which had an honest sheriff, Lamar Potts. Sheriff Potts was considered a man of integrity and was respected by everyone in Newnan, the county seat of Coweta County. Residents there felt safe because of Potts, and the county had the lowest crime rate in Georgia.

When Potts investigated the crime scene at the motel, he found that there were eight Black people who'd witnessed the killing and said they saw the way Wallace had tried to hide the murder. Potts called the sheriff in Greenville, the county seat, and asked him to send Wallace back to Newnan.

Wallace controlled politics in Meriwether and was best friends with Sheriff Hardy Collier. Collier refused to extradite him and tried to shield Wallace from being charged with the crime. Wallace must have believed he could get away with the crime in his home county. But Sheriff Potts would not agree with this deception. He told Collier, "If you don't send him back to me, I'll come up and arrest him myself."

Sheriff Collier still refused to help Potts, so Potts had to find Wallace himself. He did and then arrested and charged him with the crime. Over many months, Collier tried to sabotage the investigation against Wallace. Potts worked over several months to find Turner's body. With no body, it would be hard to make a case against Wallace. Finally, with help from a soothsayer and psychic named Mayhayley Lancaster, a box which contained some of Turner's bones was discovered.

Potts presented this evidence to a jury, who found Wallace guilty. The judge sentenced him to the electric chair. In Wallace's last words, he still claimed he was innocent of the killing of John Turner.

The trial was covered by the *Atlanta Journal-Constitution*. It was also posted on the Associated Press wire and became a national story.

In 1976, Coweta native Margaret Anne Barnes authored the book *Murder in Coweta County*, which covers the murder, investigation, trial, sentencing, and execution of John Wallace. The book was a bestseller, and Barnes received the Edgar Allan Poe Special Award for outstanding crime book from the Mystery Writers of America. The book is still being used by colleges and universities all over the country in sociology courses and law studies. Some of the press comments on the book include this quote from the *Boston Herald*: "This not-to-miss story, vividly and compellingly [brings] the small-town South to life as dramatically as some of the pages of Faulkner and Welty." The *Newport News Daily Press* said it was "spellbinding the way Margaret Anne Barnes tells this true story....Margaret Anne Barnes provides a chillingly realistic reconstruction of both the crime and the brilliant investigation that brought this culprit to justice. The atmosphere and social structure of rustic

Georgia in 1948 come alive in this fascinating book while the actions and attitudes of the resident's leap from the pages with a stunning authenticity."

The book was made into a major motion picture in 1983. It was aired as a CBS series starring Johnny Cash as Sheriff Potts; his wife, June Carter, as Mayhayley Lancaster; and Andy Griffith as John Wallace. The movie was a true depiction of the events that led to the murder of William Turner and the attempted cover-up. Griffith was known for playing a nice, sweet sheriff in the television series *The Andy Griffith Show*, but in this movie, Griffith plays John Wallace's character as the mean, vicious person he was in real life. *Murder in Coweta County* was a major hit and is still streaming.

The last paragraph in Barnes's book is a testament to Sheriff Potts: "And so, it went for than a quarter of a century. Lamar Potts became a legend in his own time and a strength to his people. He was sheriff of Coweta County for 32 years."

Barnes wrote two other books, *The Tragedy and the Triumph of Phoenix City, Alabama* and *A Buzzard Is My Best Friend*. Barnes was added to the University of Georgia's Hall of Fame, the state's highest honor. She died on October 11, 2007, at the age of eighty.

18

MARVIN GRIFFIN

Governors Marvin Griffin and Lester Maddox and Sheriff Tom Poppell: Resistance to Change

In 1954, the U.S. Supreme Court's decision in *Brown v. the Board of Education* overturned laws segregating schools and other institutions in America. Before 1954, courts passed a law that said schools and public facilities could be "separate but equal." The net effect of these laws kept Black Americans from gaining the civil rights afforded them by the U.S. Constitution.

Georgia Governor Marvin Griffin and later segregationist Governo Lester Maddox both worked to defy the court ruling. Griffin declared, "There would be no mixing of races in public schools as long I am governor." Governor Maddox declared that integration was a communist plot that was "ungodly, un-Christian and un-American."

More resistance to desegregation came from small towns, including those in McIntosh County, where Sheriff Tom Poppell ran a corrupt administration designed to keep Black citizens from voting. Poppell ran the county with an iron fist, and his oppressive office was riddled with bribery, racial discrimination, and abuses of power.

In the fall of 1957, riots broke out as nine Black students tried to enroll in Central High School in Little Rock, Arkansas. In Georgia, eighty white pastors took on segregationists in the Deep South. United Methodist ministers Bevel Jones and Candler Budd put together the "Ministers' Manifesto," an appeal for peace when Georgia decided to close schools rather than allow Black and white children to attend school together. The manifesto reads, in part, "Hatred and scorn for those of another race can never be justified. It is

Left: Marvin Griffin. *Neely Young, Georgia Made.*

Below: Lester Maddox. *Neely Young, Georgia Made.*

only as we approach our problems in a spirit of mutual respect that we can find a way to a cooperative solution of our problems."

Rabbi Jacob Rothschild from the Atlanta Jewish Temple embraced the statement from the local Christian community. On October 12, 1958, white KKK members detonated fifty sticks of dynamite in front of the temple, creating a massive hole. The temple bombing sent a shockwave through the Atlanta community. Christian leaders reissued the manifesto and were joined by Black churches; they urged the community to send money and other support to the temple. Business owners and regular citizens, including children, veterans, and widows, sent money to help rebuild the facility. Rabbi Rothschild received more than five thousand letters and postcards from around the country, and he helped the temple forge a close relationship with the Black and white Christian community which remains today.

In 1986, Governor Earnest Vandiver ran his campaign, pledging, "No not one Black child should be able to attend a white public school." When he came into office, he changed his position and established policies ending segregation in the state. He commissioned respected banker John Sibley to hold rallies all over the state to take the issue before the people. He found that most Georgians accepted his stance to have the state's public schools integrated.

In Savannah, white Mayor Malcom Maclean formed a "Committee of 100," which united white and Black leaders to march down Main Street to support the integration of schools and businesses in the city. In Albany, Black and white leaders organized the Albany Movement, which removed all segregation statutes from the books of the city.

Atlanta Mayor William Hartsfield chose Herbert Jenkins as his chief of police. While other cities in the South, including Birmingham, Alabama, sent police dogs to attack Black protesters, Chief Jenkins took the opposite approach and brokered a smooth, orderly transition to integrate public schools and businesses in Atlanta.

And in McIntosh County, grassroots organizations were formed, and Black residents began asserting their rights more aggressively. The editor of the *Darien News*, Charles Williamson, wrote stories exposing Poppell's abuses. Alliances that were formed between white and Black citizens became stronger and more common. When supporters of Poppell tried to burn Williamson's newspaper building, Williamson pressured county officials to be more effective in fighting the problems brought on by the sheriff. When Poppell was removed from office, schools, churches, and parks became more open to all citizens, and the old segregation norms slowly eroded.

In Macon, Federal Judge Augustus "Gus" Bootle was famous for his legal decisions, which helped other cities and counties in the state follow the law. When someone asked him, "Was it hard to let Blacks in Georgia schools?" Bootle said, "It was not hard at all. It was easy. Right is right."

Georgia's efforts became an inspiration that helped other states in the South agree "right is right."

19

THE HISTORY OF MOONSHINE

Moonshine Stills, Whiskey Trippers, and the Beginning of NASCAR

It all started in 1791: Congress passed the Whiskey Tax to help pay off national debts from the Revolutionary War. Farmers in Western Pennsylvania resented the tax, which they felt was unfair and burdensome. Many refused to pay and started a violent rebellion over the tax.

In 1794, a group of rebels burned the home of the Tax Supervisor John Neville. Across the region, tax collectors were tarred and feathered, and those who supported the tax were threatened with the same treatment.

President George Washington was worried that the rebellion would spread to other states, so he sent a force of thirteen thousand troops to stop the protests. When the rebels saw Washington's reaction to their actions, they returned home without a major confrontation. The unpopular Whiskey Tax was finally abolished in the early 1800s.

After the Civil War ended and Robert E. Lee surrendered, the U.S. government needed tax money to help fund the military. The government formed the Internal Revenue Service to collect tax on what they consider "luxuries," which included liquor.

Many Georgia farmers distilled homemade liquor called "moonshine" and refused to pay the tax. The most infamous of these moonshiners were two brothers, Thomas and Eli Field. They organized a way to fight the government agents, or "revenuers," who were tasked with tracking down moonshine operations. The Fields called their group the "Honest Man's Friend and Protector Group." It was a violent crime and vigilante organization that terrorized any informants who cooperated with the revenuers. The Fields' group started a moonshine war against the revenuers

Moonshine still. *Author's collection.*

that became so violent, the U.S. military was called in. The war was ended soon after, but the moonshiners still evaded and fought revenuers. In 1878, the Posse Comitatus Act was passed by Congress, which stipulated the Army could not interfere in civilian affairs. This was the positive result of the moonshine wars.

At the beginning of the twentieth century, Henry Ford's Model T changed everything. As cars became faster, it was easier to move illegal moonshine down the Georgia mountains into Atlanta. Moonshiners would have their automobiles raised up in the rear so moonshine whiskey would be poured into hollow tubs to make the car level. This new method of transporting illegal corn liquor made it more difficult for IRS agents and local sheriffs to catch moonshiners.

In 1920, the temperance movement advocated for complete abstinence from the consumption of liquor. The movement was widely supported and succeeded in bringing about the Eighteenth Amendment and Prohibition, which prevented the manufacture, sale, and transport of alcoholic beverages in the United States. The law also instigated a crime wave that lasted from 1920 until the law was repealed in 1933.

Many Americans were willing to drink liquor illegally. This was the high point of the bootlegging industry. Churches asked their members to sign a pledge card that promised they would refrain from drinking alcohol. They signed the pledge—but had their fingers crossed. Congregants created special closets to hide their liquor from their preachers when they visited.

Many towns had speakeasies, illegal secretive drinking clubs. While Chicago gangster Al Capone received all the publicity in the national press, many local Georgians and other Southerners opened similar speakeasies in their towns and cities. Al Capone was tried and convicted for tax evasion and was sentenced to serve time in Atlanta's federal prison, located near the modern-day Atlanta Zoo.

Georgia was one of the largest centers of the production of illegal spirits. It was easy to set up a still. One only needed to find a small stream in the backwoods and then buy copper piping, a large pot, sugar, and a large bag of corn. The water would be boiled in a heated pot, and then the corn would be boiled to form a mash. During this process, starches in the grain were broken down into sugars, and then the sugars would turn into alcohol. The process could be sped up by adding more sugar, yeast, and malt. The fermented mash required the additional step of separating it from the water and heating it to a proper temperature. Then it was transported by copper pipes into another pot. There, it was reconverted back to a liquid. Peaches and other fruits were added to flavor the final distilled product, which would then be poured into whiskey bottles and transferred to a waiting car that would drive it to Atlanta to be distributed to illegal stores.

During the 1920s and 1930s, IRS agents and local sheriffs seized 340,000 stills and arrested 1 million men. Georgia led every other state in the number of stills seized by agents.

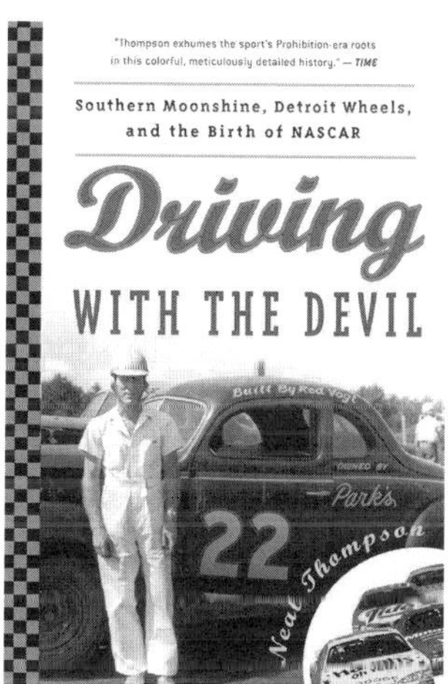

Driving with the Devil, by Neal Thompson. *Three Rivers Press*, 2006.

Federal agents would cover the highways to arrest those driving down to cities and towns in their aggressive pursuit of untaxed whiskey. But the moonshiners' cars were fast and driven by bootlegger "trippers," who were adept at escaping agents. Many lives were lost in these chases, including those of moonshine producers, trippers, and agents.

This war prompted a mutual respect between the moonshiners and IRS agents in many communities. Sometimes, revenuers would capture a tripper, but if they knew their family, they'd let them go. And families were known to name their newborn children after revenuers.

NASCAR today. *Author's collection.*

Songs like "Thunder Road" tell the story of both moonshiners' and sheriffs' efforts to keep the law or break it. Many funny stories populate the history of these times.

One story is the "Tale of a Mule":

> *One fine Georgia evening Mrs. Bill Wood called a veterinarian who lived in Peach County. She was upset and said, "Doctor, my mule, Buck, is sick. Can you look at him?"*
>
> *The doctor told the woman that he was eating supper and did not want to drive out to look after a mule. He told her to give him a dose of mineral oil, and if that did not work, he would come in the morning.*
>
> *She wanted to know how to give the mule the mineral oil, and he told her to give it through a funnel and "it's best given not in his mouth but at the other end."*
>
> *Mrs. Wood found a fox hunting horn and placed it into Buck's back end. But she could not find any mineral oil. Instead, she found some red-hot turpentine and pored it into the horn. Buck stood still for a few moments then let out squeal that was heard a mile down the road. He cleared a fence and ran down the road at a mad gallop. He was in great pain and his rear end jumped up and down every few seconds. Every time he jumped, the horn would blow.*
>
> *All the hound dogs in the neighborhood thought the mule was being readied for a fox hunt. So, out down the road they went running after Buck,*

> *barking joyously! The sight was something to see: a mule racing down the road, horn blowing and dogs yapping.*
>
> *It was getting dark when Buck and the dogs came to the river. They dove into the river and swam to the other side. The river keeper heard the horn blowing and the dogs barking and saw a fast boat coming. He drew up the bridge and let the boat go by.*
>
> *The bridge tender was also the county sheriff, and he was running for re-election. He lost the race and only got a few votes. People figured that any man who did not know the difference between a mule with a horn up his caboose and a boat coming down the river was not fit to hold any public office in the county.*

Prohibition was abolished in 1933 and was replaced by a new law, which made sure taxes were collected successfully. It mandated a three-tier system, which separated producer, distributer, and retailer in collecting state and federal taxes. This law put an end to the moonshine industry all over the United States.

During the days of whiskey delivery, many trippers would gather for drag racing contests to see who had the fastest car. The races would be attended by large crowds that would bet on who would win the contest. This was the beginning of modern-day NASCAR. In the 1930s, dirt track events were called stock car races, grown out of running moonshine during Prohibition.

In 1948, a private company founded by Jim France helped these auto racing events go mainstream. Today, the National Association for Stock Car Auto Racing (NASCAR) is a top-ranked motor sports organization. NASCAR sanctions over 1,500 races on over 100 tracks in 48 states and in Europe, Canada, Mexico, and Brazil. Richard Petty holds the record of having the most wins with 200. Dale Earnhardt and Jimmy Johnson are tied for having the most championship records. Sports TV and legal sports betting rights make NASCAR.com one of the top sport viewing venues in the world.

NASCAR has had to deal with safety issues, much like the moonshine drivers in the old days. One driver, Fireball Roberts, was killed when flames engulfed his car during a race. The deaths of Adam Petty, Kenny Irwin, and Tony Roper initiated the requirement of fire-retardant suits for drivers and a kill-switch throttle. After the death of Dale Earnhardt, NASCAR has become more aggressive with its safety changes. Since 2024, no driver has been killed in an accident.

The history of the whiskey wars, moonshiners, revenuers, trippers, mule stories, and NASCAR has been quite a ride. It is as old as America itself.

20

THE ROSWELL WOMEN

Sherman's Disgrace

This is the true story of what happened to four hundred women who were brutally treated during General William Tecumseh Sherman's Battle of Atlanta during the Civil War.

On June 27, 1864, Sherman was already halfway through the state, near Atlanta, and he was burning and destroying homes, towns, and crops as he went. There is a story, which is not true, that claims he said, "War is hell, and I will make it so." But it *is* true that he said, "I will make Georgia howl."

Sherman was at Kennesaw Mountain, near Marietta, when he was stopped by Confederate forces. He had his first defeat there at the south end of the battle, which was called the "Dead Angle." Sherman sent his troops up a steep slope, where they were decimated by the Confederate infantry. It was one of the deadliest days of the battle, when the Union army lost three thousand men in just a few hours.

The Southern army was greatly outnumbered and moved across the river to Atlanta while Sherman had to find another way to cross the river. Sherman sent Brigadier General Kenner Garrard to find a new way across the Chattahoochee River. Garrard arrived in Roswell, located just an hour northeast of Marietta.

Roswell had some of the most attractive antebellum homes in the state. It contained the summer homes of wealthy residents who tried to escape the summer heat of Savannah and coastal Georgia. One famous home was the residence of James Bullock and his daughter, Mattie. In 1852, Mattie

Roswell Mills. *Roswell Historical Society.*

married Theodore Roosevelt Sr., and they became the parents of President Theodore Roosevelt. Roswell was also a mill town that made uniforms for the Confederate army. When Garrard's troops entered the town, they discovered three mills: a wool mill and two cotton mills. The mills manufactured sheeting, tent canvas, and rope. Most importantly, the third mill produced the gray-colored cloth that was used to make Confederate uniforms. The mills were in full operation and were staffed by hundreds of women and young girls. Many brought their children to work with them because they could take care of them on-site. Many of Roswell's residents had left town before the army arrived, but the mill workers remained on the job.

One of the structures had a French flag flying outside. A Frenchman, Theophile Roach, was the owner of the factory and hoped the flag would save his mill. But Garrard found the Confederate symbol "CSA" stamped all over the clothes. When he reported this to Sherman, the general ordered Garrard to burn the mills and arrest the women and children for treason. Garrard was directed to give the workers nine days' worth of rations and ship them north across the Ohio River.

Garrard was reluctant to obey these harsh orders. Sherman wrote in response:

> *In the Field, near Chattahoochee River:*
> *General, I assure you, in spite of any little disappointment I may have expressed, I feel for you personally not only respect but affection, and wish for your unmeasured success and reputation, but I do wish to inspire all cavalry with my conviction that caution and prudence should be but a small element in their characters.*
>
> *I repeat my orders that you arrest all people, male and female, connected to those factories, no matter what the clamor, and let them foot it, under guard, to Marietta, whence I will send them by cars to the North.*
>
> *The poor women will make a howl. Let them take along their children and clothing, provided they have the means of hauling, or you can spare them.*
>
> *In your next letter, give me as much information as you can as to the size and dimension of the burned bridge.*
>
> *W.T. SHERMAN, Major General, Commanding*

Sherman noted that the women were "tainted with treason" and "are as much governed by the rules of war as if in the ranks, the whole region was devoted to manufacturing, but I will destroy every one of them."

General Gerrard had the women placed in wagons for a short trip to Marietta. There, they were quartered at the Georgia Military Institute, which had been abandoned by the fleeing Southern troops. On July 15, the women were placed in boxcars and given a few days' worth of food. They were bound to Louisville, Kentucky, the final destination for many of the mill workers. The women were fed and sent to a refugee hospital and then were turned out to find living quarters on their own. The women had no way to write their husbands to let them know where they were.

Some of the women were sent to Ohio. When they were let off the train, they had to find places to stay. They struggled to find work because they knew only how to spin yarn in a mill. So, they had to find work wherever they could. The women knew they would never be able to find their way back home. Many who survived after the war remarried and stayed in the North.

A reporter from the *New York Tribune*, Harry Newman, heard the great wail from the women who were being driven to the city. He sent a dispatch

Top, left: The grave of Adeline Bagley, a Roswell Mill worker. *Author's collection.*

Top, right: General William Tecumseh Sherman. *Matthew Brady, Library of Congress.*

Bottom: Monument to the Roswell Women. *Author's collection.*

to his editor that read, "Only think of it! Four hundred weeping and terrified Ellens, Susans and Maggies transported in the seatless and springless army, away from their lovers and brothers of the sunny South, and all this for the offense of weaving tent cloth and spinning yard."

Newman's piece became a major story in newspapers across the North. The women at the institute had no idea of the furor churning on their account. One example came from the *New York Commercial*:

> *A new correspondent published a story, which, we trust, for the sake of the officer implicated, as well as our own good national name, may prove to be unfounded. It is to the effect that General Sherman, finding in Roswell, Georgia, four hundred factory girls, employed in a large cotton factory, at that point, ordered the whole of the unfortunate creatures to be sent north to Ohio.*
>
> *General Sherman has shown on two or three occasions that his ability as a military commander is quite compatible with something not far removed from imbecility in respect to civil matters. He writes stupendously foolish orders on things political and is evidently incapable of administering a village on practical principal.*
>
> *But it is hardly conceivable that an officer, wearing the United States commission of Major General, should so far have forgotten the commonest dictates of decency and humanity (Christian apart), as to drive four hundred penniless girls to seek a livelihood amid a strange and hostile people.*
>
> *We repeat our most earnest hope that further information may redeem the name of General Sherman and our one from the frightful disgrace which this story, as it comes to us, must inflict upon one or the other.*

There is no record of how this uproar in the North effected Sherman, but his actions did not change when he later sent his army on its infamous March to the Sea.

In 1998, the Sons of Confederate Veterans worked on a project to find the victims of the Roswell women relocation and their descendants. Their efforts found many of the families. In July 2000, the city of Roswell erected a monument to honor the four hundred Roswell Mill women.

21

WILLIAM SIMMONS

The Arrival of the Ku Klux Klan in 1915

On November 25, 1915, William Simmons and fifteen of his followers climbed Stone Mountain near Atlanta in white robes with hoods covering their faces. They burned a large cross and inaugurated the second incarnation of the Ku Klux Klan. The "impressive service" event was described as a social party in an article in the *Atlanta Journal-Constitution* on November 28.

The first iteration of the Ku Klux Klan was formed just after the Civil War to suppress federal influence during Reconstruction. This second Klan was formed by Simmons to promote violence against Black, Jewish, and Catholic people. Later, in the 1950s, a third incarnation of the Klan focused on opposing the civil rights movement.

William Simmons was a so-called Christian preacher, and his Klan flourished in the 1915s and early 1920s and grew to have over four million national members. The movie *The Birth of a Nation* glorifies the Ku Klux Klan's early days and influenced Simmons. He used the trial and hanging of Leo Frank as a tool to recruit white people to his cause. Simmons wanted to proclaim that the Klan's goal was to support white supremacy and protect white people's rights as so-called "pure Americans."

At first, the KKK maintained it was a nonviolent organization, but it soon became a group that advocated for violence against Black people and other minorities. Many cities, like Macon, had a Black population that made up more than 40 percent of their populations overall. White citizens were worried that this number of Black residents was a threat to their city. They welcomed the KKK and asked the group to put Black residents "in their place." The secret order wore white-hooded costumes and burned crosses in the front yards of ministers and other leaders, both white and Black, in the community.

KKK members in costume. *Author's collection.*

In 1912, the KKK marched in Forsyth County, a community just north of Atlanta that has a long history of violence carried out against Black residents. A white woman was murdered, and the prime suspect was a Black man housed in the city's jail. Even though the man was in jail at the time of the murder, a white mob broke into his cell and killed him. The sheriff and police officers remained silent, and no arrests were made. Other Black citizens were hanged, and people of color were chased out of the county. White residents raised a sign in the city that read, "Blacks Are Not Welcome Here."

Over the years, many other KKK attacks and cross burnings occurred all over the nation. The Midwestern states had the largest memberships in the Klan. City and county governments and police were reluctant to challenge the Klan's brutally. Those who did were targeted with more savage action.

Klan membership was at its peak in the 1920s; during the 1930s, Georgia's membership declined from 150,000 to only 1,400. The KKK's national membership went from 5 million to less that 30,000. It was disbanded in the 1940s. However, during the civil rights movement of the 1950s and '60s, the KKK experienced a resurgence. One example of these new members was Georgia racist J.B. Stoner.

Stoner was a poster boy for racial extremism in the United States. He was born on April 13, 1924, in Walker County, Georgia's northwest county closest to the Tennessee border. The town's main city is named Lafayette in honor of the Marquises de Lafayette, who aided Georgia Washington during the Revolutionary War. The region was settled by the Scotch-Irish, and its mountain residents are considered independent and mistrustful of any government or authority.

As a young man, Stoner contracted polio and walked with a limp for the rest of his life. It was believed his fear of Black and Jewish people began at that time. As a teen, he joined the Ku Klux Klan. He stalked Reverend Dr.

Martin Luther King Jr. and attended rallies to protest King's policies of changing attitudes in the segregated South. Later, he was on the legal team that tried to appeal James Earl Ray's conviction after King's murder.

Stoner graduated from the Atlanta Law School in 1945 and set up his practice in Marietta. There, he painted a large sign on the wall outside his office that promoted segregation between white and Black people. He changed the sign often to promote his hateful slogans and his views on Jewish people. In 1958, there were a series of bombings at Black churches across the South, and Stoner was believed to be one of the men involved. However, he was not charged with the crimes.

Stoner helped form the National States' Rights Party, and in 1964, he ran for vice president on the national ticket, receiving only 6,980 votes out of the 70 million cast. He then ran for governor in 1970 as a candidate for the Anti-Semitic Party. He said Black people belonged to a branch of the ape family and that Jews were "vipers of hell."

Domestic terrorism: cross burning. *Author's collection.*

In his campaign speeches, he said that he was the candidate of love, that he loved white people and white children. He was defeated by Jimmy Carter, the future president of the United States.

Two years later, Stoner ran for the U.S. Senate against Sam Nunn. During the campaign, Stoner won a ruling that said he could keep running advertisements that used racial epithets for Black people. Stoner received only forty thousand votes and lost to Nunn.

In 1974, Stoner ran for lieutenant governor. He said Hitler was too moderate and that they should have left him alone. Surprisingly, he received 10 percent of the vote.

In 1977, while campaigning for governor, he was arrested and indicted on charges of bombing Bethel Church in Birmingham, Alabama, in 1958. The church served as the headquarters of the Alabama Christian Movement for Human Rights. Because of the church's visibility in the fight for integration, segregationists targeted it. Officials suspected Stoner was involved in more than a dozen other church bombings. He was convicted in 1980 and was sentenced to ten years' imprisonment. He served for only three years before he was paroled for good behavior.

Stoner lived for another twenty-five years but never ran for political office again. He died on April 23, 2005, at the age of eighty-one. He passed away still believing that those of the white Anglo-Saxon race were God's chosen people.

After the integration of schools and other institutions following the civil rights movement, the balance of the twentieth century became relatively peaceful and democratic between Black and white Americans. The twenty-first century has seen the rise of similar KKK-type organizations.

22

TOM WATSON AND LEO FRANK

How the Hanging of Leo Frank Changed Georgia's Approach to Racial Justice

"Georgia On My Mind" is a song that signals to the world that the state is racially tolerant and welcomes citizens of all colors and religions. This attitude is the main reason the state has enjoyed explosive economic growth over the past sixty years. Today, Georgia's economic development has outstripped, by a wide margin, that of its fellow Southern states. And this fantastic success is mostly owed to business leaders who stepped up and took courageous actions during the civil rights movement of the late 1950s and '60s.

Georgia was not always so welcoming. In the early part of the twentieth century, Georgia, along with other Southern states, was nationally known as a racist, bigoted, and dangerous place for people of color. This was highlighted in 1915 by the Leo Frank case, in which a Jewish man in Atlanta was placed on trial and unjustly convicted of raping and murdering a thirteen-year-old girl named Mary Phagan.

Frank was the head of the National Pencil Company, where Phagan worked. On April 26, 1913, Frank was working in his office when Phagan came to ask for her wages. Later that afternoon, a watchman discovered her body at the rear of the factory's basement. Initially, police suspected Phagan had been killed by the man who found her body, but their suspicions soon turned toward Frank. He was arrested and charged with the crime.

Tom Watson was a populist politician and editor of the weekly *Jeffersonian Magazine*. His newspaper ran daily sensational headlines about the trial, portraying Frank as a "lewd, loathsome Jew." The paper also urged the jury to find Frank guilty of the murder.

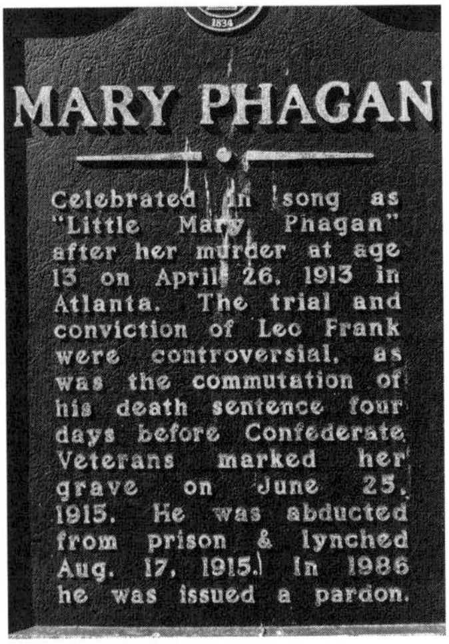

Mary Phagan historical marker. *Author's collection.*

After the jury found Frank guilty, Governor John M. Slaton examined the evidence; he decided there was no proof of Frank's guilt and said he had been convicted because he was Jewish. Slaton changed Frank's sentence from death to life in prison. Slaton's decision enraged the public, and there were riots all over the state. Martial law was declared, and the National Guard was called in to help control the melee.

Watson's newspaper fanned the flames of public opinion by asking that a vigilante mob overturn Slaton's action. On the night of August 16, a group of citizens from Marietta, Mary Phagan's hometown, took Frank from his cell, drove him to Marietta, and hanged him from an oak tree.

The lynching of Leo Frank was a highly publicized national story that exposed to the world Georgia's shameful treatment of Jewish people, Black people, and other minorities. Soon afterward, there was a revival of the infamous Ku Klux Klan, with its white hoods, cross burning, and lynchings of Black people all over the South. Georgia was part of this system for many dark years and did not alter its course until a dramatic change, helped by business and religious leaders, began to take shape in the late 1950s.

At the same time, Alabama Governor George Wallace was standing at the University of Alabama's front door saying "No" and using his state patrol to block Black students from entering the university. Later, Birmingham presented an ugly national picture when vicious guard dogs and strong fire hoses were turned on Black protesters.

In dramatic contrast, Georgia's Governor Earnest Vandiver ordered the state patrol to protect two Black students, Hamilton Holmes and Charlayne Hunter, when they entered the University of Georgia. Vandiver then appointed a state commission headed by Trust Company of Georgia banker John Sibley to help prepare the rest of the state for court-ordered school desegregation. More that 1,800 Georgians appeared at statewide hearings. Most people credited the committee with convincing citizens that it was time for a change. The commission's hearing "broke a freeze of fear and silence," wrote Gene Patterson, the then-editor of the *Atlanta Journal-*

Constitution. As a result of the commission's findings, Vandiver convinced the general assembly to repeal an earlier law that banned the use of state funds to integrate schools.

A similar acceptance of integration began to occur all over Georgia. In Savannah, nonviolent demonstrations and calls for a boycott of racist white merchants were held. An influential "Committee of 100" white business and community leaders stood with Black leaders and walked together into Savannah's segregated facilities, which soon changed their policies. Savannah was desegregated some eight months ahead of the federal Civil Rights Act, which was passed during the Johnson administration.

In Albany, Georgia, activist Frances Pauley, who was white, worked to unite Black and white leaders in what is now known as the Albany Movement. To help with this effort, the Black community called in Reverend Dr. Martin Luther King Jr. and other prominent civil rights leaders, including Andrew Young. The Albany Movement was tasked with joining white business and political leaders with their counterparts in the Black community. By bridging the two groups, Pauley helped bring success and, after some time, a peaceful integration of these communities.

Atlanta's Mayor Ivan Allan successfully won an election challenge against arch-segregationist Lester Maddox, as Atlanta voters embraced his strong stand for the civil rights of all citizens. He was able to marshal a coalition of Black and white business leaders, including important people like the late Black businessman Herman Russell. Atlanta was the home of national leader Reverend Dr. Martin Luther King Jr., and some have said that King's positive relationship with Atlanta's local business and community leaders, both Black and white, helped give him the knowledge and strong leadership he needed to become a national leader of the civil rights movement.

Alabama and the city of Birmingham are different today because they changed their attitudes on civil rights, but the brutal treatment of Alabama's Black citizens during segregation gave the state a bad reputation that has been hard to overcome. In the census of 1950, Birmingham had a population of 445,000; Atlanta was similarly sized, with 507,000 residents. Since that time, Birmingham has barely grown and has a population of only 749,000, while Atlanta now has 4.5 million citizens and Georgia has grown to have over 10 million citizens, almost triple its 1950 population.

Many other events over the past sixty years have propelled Georgia to become the economic powerhouse it is today, including the construction of the Hartsfield-Jackson International Airport and Georgia's ports, the introduction of major league sports teams, and Atlanta's hosting of the 1996 Olympics. But the willingness of Georgia's business community to stand with others to promote social issues, including the acceptance of all races as equal, has been the cornerstone of the state's success. "Georgia On My Mind" still has the same meaning for the state today.

23

THE TRAIL OF TEARS

How Indian Chief John Ridge Sold Out the Cherokee Nation and Spurred the Trail of Tears

The removal of the Cherokee in 1838 is one of the more shameful events in the history of America. Called the "Trail of Tears," some historians estimate that more than four thousand women, children, and men perished during the march from Georgia, Tennessee, and North Carolina to a new land in Oklahoma. One of the questions of history is: Why did the United States mistreat the Natives so horribly?

Historians have wondered how many Natives lived in the Americas before Columbus. The United Nations estimates the world's population was 500 million in the sixteenth century. Historian James Mooney estimates the North American Native population was 1.5 million. Yet at the time of the Cherokees' removal, the United States' Native population had already been reduced by almost 90 percent. What happened?

The 1500s spawned a century of epidemics, including the Black Death and the plague, diseases which killed one out of every five people on earth. When Hernando de Soto landed with his army in Florida in 1539, he brought three hundred pigs with him. During the next four years, he wandered through Florida, Georgia, North and South Carolina, Alabama, Mississippi, Arkansas, Texas, and Louisiana looking for gold and torturing and killing countless Natives. But the worst thing he did was bring the pigs.

Natives did not live with their livestock, unlike Europeans, who lived around their livestock and became immune to the diseases they carried. When pigs and horses were brought to the Americas, the Native population had no such immunity, and hundreds of thousands of Natives all over the

John Ridge. *Neely Young, Georgia Made.*

Southeast died from diseases that had been carried in by the Europeans' pigs, including tuberculosis and smallpox. For example, in the society of the Caddo, located on the Texas-Arkansas border, the Native population fell from about 200,000 to about 8,500, a drop of nearly 90 percent, according to Timothy Perttula, an archaeological consultant in Austin. He estimates that the Native population in the Coosa area in Georgia fell by the same amount.

When James Oglethorpe settled Georgia in 1733, the area's Native population was decimated. If the Native population had remained as large as it once was, the European conquest of the Americas would have been much more difficult.

Another problem for the Natives was that in early wars, they picked the wrong side—three times. They sided against the English in the French and Indian War (1754–1763) and against the Americans in the Revolutionary War in 1776 and the War of 1812. In the first war, when the English fought the French, the Natives picked the French, thus the name the French and Indian War. Two generations later, the Natives sided with the British against the Americans during the Revolutionary War.

During the Revolutionary War, a British officer was sent a package from Native tribes, which bragged about the prizes they had captured during a raid on a white American settlement. It contained the hands, feet, and scalps of women, children, and colonial soldiers. The ghoulish relics were described in a letter: "One box containing 102 farmers that were burned alive, 81 women, 193 boys' scalps of various ages, 211 girls' scalps, mixture 122 containing with box containing 29 infant scalps. Only a little black knife in middle to show they were ripped out of mother's body." The news of the discovery of this awful package spread all over the colonies and did much to form opinions that later influenced white Americans' negative picture of the entire Native population.

During the War of 1812, the Natives picked the wrong side for the third time. Fueled by an 1811 visit from the great warrior Tecumseh, who wanted to form an Indian Federation of all the tribes east of the Mississippi, the Creek in lower Georgia and throughout most of Alabama led a bloody revolt. They raided and killed many white settlers along both sides of the Chattahoochee River. Yet many of the Cherokee in North Georgia sided with the Americans during this conflict. The Creek warriors were worried that the recent construction of the Federal Road through Georgia and Alabama would bring more white settlers into what had once been Native wilderness. William Weatherford, a half Scot–half Native chief of the Creeks, formed a band called the Red Sticks, named for the bright paint they applied to their war clubs, and engineered a savage war on white settlers in the region. In 1811, Weatherford's war party of 700 braves attacked Fort Mims, near Mobile, Alabama. They tomahawked, scalped and mutilated 175 white settlers, including women and children.

Andrew Jackson came down from Tennessee with an army to hunt down Weatherford and put an end to the war of the Red Sticks. Jackson prevailed at the Battle of Horseshoe Bend in southern Alabama on March 27, 1814. Jackson then moved his army to New Orleans, where he won a battle against the British as the War of 1812 came to an end.

The nail in the coffin for the Cherokee Nation came after the war, when gold was discovered at what is now Villa Rica, west of Atlanta near Carrolton. White speculators now had a bull's-eye on the land of the Cherokee. When Jackson became president, the "Indian Removal" issue took center stage. Jackson's 1829 oration called on Congress to enact a federal law for the removal of Natives, and on May 28, 1830, the Indian Removal Act was signed into law. The removal was, in theory, optional: The Natives could stay or move west. But great pressure was placed on tribes to sign removal treaties.

The Cherokee population in North Georgia in 1832 was estimated to be around 13,500. Over the generations since Columbus's arrival in

America, European settlers had intermarried with the Native population. Most Cherokee now had a mixed white and Native heritage. Two Cherokee leaders took center stage. One was John Ross, an educated white man with a Native background who was elected chief of the Cherokee in 1828. His home was located close to Rome and still stands today. Major John Ridge, the son of a Scottish trader and Native mother, also became an influential player at this time and was appointed by Jackson to be a counselor to the Cherokee Nation.

Ross strongly opposed the cession of Native lands, even though the federal government had obtained a great deal of Cherokee lands over decades. Throughout Ridge's military career, he served as a diplomat to Washington, D.C., for both the Cherokee and the Creeks. Ridge believed the Cherokee cause was hopeless and was working to find a way the Cherokee could move west from Georgia. Ross was the principal chief of the Cherokee National Council, and Ridge headed up a faction called the Treaty Party. Between the two points of view, there were heated arguments, animosities, and some violence, which split the Cherokee population.

Enter Georgia Governor William Lumpkin (1831–1835). Lumpkin became fed up with the federal government's waiting game regarding the Cherokees' removal. He had the territory surveyed and then divided into ten counties. Between 1832 and 1833, the territory was dispensed to qualified drawers in a lottery, and after the lottery, Lumpkin continued to support the removal of the Cherokee from the state.

After the lottery of 1832, when white people began moving into Cherokee lands to either settle or to look for gold, hostilities between the Natives and the newcomers reached new highs.

Finally, the federal government and the Cherokee came to an agreement, and the Treaty of New Echota was signed on December 29, 1835. However, only Ridge's Treaty Party was represented at the event, as Ross's Cherokee National Council protested and refused to sign the document. The treaty's terms directed the Cherokee to cede their territory in the Southeast and move west to the Indian Territory in what is now Oklahoma.

Earlier, in Alabama, the Creek tribe, under orders from Jackson, was moved out of the state to lands west of the Mississippi. But a group of renegade Creeks went against Jackson's order and moved into Georgia, near Cedartown, where they settled with the local Cherokee. In May 1837, citizens wrote to Lumpkin asking for help to defend locals against the Native newcomers. They told Lumpkin that the Creeks were not willing to go West, and since coming to the area, they had incited the Cherokee to become more hostile than they had been before. They wrote: "The Creeks are willing to aid the Cherokee in killing up the white people and taking their lands. They continued robbing and plundering our citizens ever since they came here, and we do assure your Excellency that, unless the Creek Indians are speedily removed from this country, our honest white citizens must either remove from the country or submit to savage ambition and violence." The letter was signed by ten local white citizens.

Lumpkin took immediate action and wrote to U.S. Secretary of War Lewis Cass, saying that if the federal government failed to act, "I shall take proper steps to put in a speedy requisition for such a militia force."

Lumpkin's term came to an end in 1835, and he was succeeded by Augusta native William Schley, who related to the Eves. Schley County is named after this governor, who was responsible for keeping the peace before the Cherokee removal's final effort.

Soon after Schley's election in 1835, the federal government moved the more than willing Ridge and his family to Honey Ridge, Oklahoma, and another two thousand Cherokee peacefully followed them to the West. But many stayed behind, and General Winfield Scott was given the official order to remove all remaining Cherokee.

As soon as the 1835 Treaty of New Echota was signed, the U.S. military started the construction of twenty collection forts all over the Cherokee Nation. The lies the American government told the Natives during this time were shameful. Almost the entirety of the Cherokee population had little knowledge of the treaty that was signed by Ridge, an agent, and not by Ross, the Cherokees' official chief.

Ross and another Cherokee leader named Whitepath heard of the treaty and were stunned. They traveled to Washington to meet with Jackson and find out if it was true the removal had been approved. The president told the chief, "You shall remain in your ancient land as long as grass grows and water runs."

In another big lie, the American government was able to convince the Cherokee Natives that the forts were not collection points for their move west but were to be the Natives' new homes in Georgia.

The removal moved full force when Scott took over the tack on May 8, 1838. There were many rumors of mistreatment of the Natives, so Scott issued orders that the Natives be treated with kindness and that the sick and elderly be given special accommodations.

By this time, Lumpkin had handed off his responsibility to the new governor, George H. Gilmer.

Scott appointed Captain John Vincent to head the federal company charged with moving the local Native population to the camps to get them ready for the trip west. Many made the trip to the camps and stockades voluntarily, but most were rounded up by squads of troops who arrived with fixed bayonets at the doorways of Native homes. Natives were seized in their fields and taken away without even a chance to say goodbye to their loved ones. Many fled as they saw their homes go up in flames. It didn't take long for local white people to move in and round up the Natives' cattle and other livestock.

September 1830 saw more than twenty-seven thousand Cherokee Natives moved by river transport and on foot west to their new home in Oklahoma. Over four thousand perished on the long eight-hundred-mile-long march; they died of starvation, exposure, and disease. Ross, who had worked so hard to remain in Georgia, made the trip; his wife died on the long journey. This is why the event is known as the "Trail of Tears."

Greed for gold and land for white expansion, racial prejudice against the Natives, and, most importantly, a fear of the militant Creek Natives who moved into Cherokee territory all combined to kill the Cherokee Nation in Georgia. Not to be ignored was the split among the Cherokee tribe concerning the move west.

Larry Carter's book *Polk County, Georgia* gives a good summary of the events of 1830. Carter writes: "It has taken historians many years to ascertain many of the circumstances, number of deaths and inhumane treatment of the Cherokee suffered when removed from Georgia. It was a forced removal conducted under threat of annihilation. The Trail of Tears cannot be described as anything but a tragic tale. And it is a tale of force winning over decency and power winning over justice. "

After the events of 1830, white Americans adopted as their own many of the virtues Natives express, those of honor, dignity, freedom, stoicism, self-sufficiency, and toughness.

24

LYNN TURNER

The Jell-O Killer

Lucia Lynn Turner was born near Atlanta in Marietta, Cobb County, on July 13, 1968. She was adopted by the Womack family, and when the Womacks divorced, she lived with her mother until she was a teenager. Her mother later discovered that Lynn was using drugs and sent her to a substance abuse clinic. Lynn was a difficult person, and the drug abuse continued until she graduated from high school.

By 1991, Lynn was employed by Cobb County as a 911 dispatcher. She wanted to become a police officer but failed the psychological exam. Lynn then met a Cobb County police officer named Glenn Turner, and the two struck up a romance. They married in Marietta in August 1992. At first, the two had a good marriage, and Glenn took an additional job at a gas station to support the couple after Lynn left her job with Cobb County. She then convinced her new husband to purchase a $150,000 life insurance policy.

Lynn loved to shop and spend, and she started buying clothes and other items Glenn could not afford. The two started having marital problems because of the excessive debt Lynn was incurring.

Soon, Lynn met a firefighter named Randy Thompson. Without her husband's knowledge, the two began having an affair. Lynn told Randy that she planned to divorce Glenn, but Glenn and Lynn patched up their marriage for a while. In secret, Lynn kept up her affair with Randy.

On March 2, 1995, Lynn served Glenn some Jell-O. Later, he fell ill and started experiencing flu-like symptoms. He went to the emergency room and was treated there. He felt better, and Lynn and Glenn went to bed for the night. When Lynn woke up the next morning, she found that Glenn had died. She called 911, and an ambulance arrived to take him to the funeral home. She told police that Glenn had a heart condition, and the Cobb County coroner ruled his death was the result of his irregular heartbeat. Soon after, Lynn collected on the $150,000 insurance policy.

Also soon after Glenn's death, Lynn moved in with Randy Thompson, and they purchased a house together. Lynn asked Randy to purchase a $200,000 life insurance policy. By 2000, Randy and Lynn were having problems in their relationship, and he wanted to move out. Lynn became a little sweeter, and things got better.

On January 22, 2001, Lynn made Randy some Jell-O. Randy started having flu-like symptoms and began vomiting. Lynn sent him to the emergency room, where he was treated and released. But by the next day, Randy Thompson, age thirty-two, was dead. His reported cause of death was an irregular heartbeat. When Lynn tried to collect on his $200,000 life insurance policy, however, she discovered it had lapsed due to delinquent payments.

Glenn Turner's mother read Randy's obituary and noticed that Randy and Glenn had died from the same problem. She called the police and asked them to reopen the case of Glenn's death. They, too, then noticed the two men had died under the same circumstances. Blood test results found ethylene glycol antifreeze in both men's systems. Before Glenn's death, Lynn had visited an animal hospital and asked the vets what kind of poisons they

Suspicious death ruled a homicide

■ Man and poisoning victim both linked to ex-Cobb 911 dispatcher

By Jeffrey Widmer
Marietta Daily Journal Staff Writer

MARIETTA — Forsyth County firefighter Randy Thompson, who died in January of antifreeze poisoning and is linked romantically to a former Cobb County 911 dispatcher, was murdered, state officials have ruled.

Dr. Mark Koponen of the Georgia Bureau of Investigation, which is investigating Thompson's death along with that of former Cobb police officer Glenn Turner, determined that the ethylene glycol found in Thompson's system had to be administered by someone.

Determining who did it could be another matter altogether.

Thompson, 32, died in January after having a relationship with Lynn Turner, 33, Turner's widow. His death was originally listed as cardiac dysrythmia, or

Glenn Turner

Lynn Turner

Turner died in 1995, just a few months after his marriage to Ms. Turner. The Cobb County Medical Examiner's Office also attributed his death to natural causes.

Turner's friends and family questioned his death from the beginning and last month, after his body was exhumed in July, tests showed antifreeze was present in his system at the time of death.

GBI investigators still are

Glenn and Lynn Turner. *Marietta Daily Journal, August 11, 2001.*

SATURDAY • AUGUST 11, 2001

In addition to the deaths of her two former husbands, Lynn Turner — who stood silently at Friday's press conference — also is being investigated in the death of former Forsyth sheriff's Maj. Ronald J. Casper, who passed away in 1999. Casper was Turner's boss, and the two were under investigation for missing funds when he died of respiratory failure.

The Associated Press

Lynn Turner. *Marietta Daily Journal, August 11, 2001.*

used to put down dogs and cats. The police subsequently found antifreeze in her garage.

Officials accused Lynn of poisoning both men by lacing their Jell-O with antifreeze. They believed that because Jell-O has a sweet taste and antifreeze is odorless, both men would not have expected the dessert to kill them.

In 2004, Lynn was arrested and charged with the murder of Glenn Turner. She was found guilty. Later, in 2010, she was found guilty of the murder of Randy Thompson. At the trial for the murder of Randy, the jury almost sentenced Lynn to death by execution, a rare sentence for a woman. But they later changed her sentence to life imprisonment without parole.

In 2007, the case was appealed to the Georgia Supreme Court. The court reviewed the case and ruled that Lynn was guilty of feeding both men Jell-O that contained antifreeze. After their deaths, Lynn had received more than $230,000 in life insurance, and the jurors named that as the motive for the murders. The court ruled that the evidence presented to the jury found no harmful error. In the case of Turner v. the State: "The Supreme Court of Georgia affirmed the Judgement, and all the justices concur."

On August 30, 2010, Lynn Turner died by suicide. A CBS TV headline told the story of her death: "Antifreeze Killer Lynn Turner Dies in Prison." In the CBS/AP story Sharmelle Brooks of the Georgia Department of Corrections said, "Lynn Turner was found 'unresponsive' Monday in her cell at Metro State Prison and could not be revived."

National media became interested in Turner's case. Her story been told many times on television. In 2007, an episode titled "Cold Hearted" aired on the show *Forensic Files*. The Oxygen Network show *Snapped* aired an episode about Turner's case that same year. The Discovery Channel aired her story on a show called *Deadly Women*. And in 2012, the ABC Show *Final Witness* told her story in an episode titled "Vixen's Elixir."

25

YAZOO LAND FRAUD

How Crooked Political Leaders Shamed Early Georgia and Caused a Landmark Federal Supreme Court Ruling

In 1732, James Oglethorpe founded the colony of Georgia. While the other colonies were formed to make many English settlers wealthy, Oglethorpe committed to establishing a new colony devoted to helping the poor and debt-ridden people of London. On January 13, 1733, a ship with 120 people sailed from London with the goal to set up the thirteenth colony in the New World. Oglethorpe founded the city of Savannah by entering into a treaty with Tomochichi, the chief of the Natives who lived there. The laws of the colony set by the trusties stated, "That no alcohol would be allowed because rum leads to idleness. No slaves will be allowed, and no Lawyers shall be allowed."

After the Revolutionary War, Georgia was expanded from a small state to include land that began at the South Carolina border and stretched all the way to the Mississippi River. This included land called the "Yazoo Lands," named for a river with the same Native name. The river is in what is now the state of Mississippi. Georgia's governor at the time, George Mathews, and U.S. Senator James Gunn devised a plan to sell these lands and line their pockets with the profits.

By 1780, all early laws set by Oglethorpe were gone. Rum and alcohol, slavery, and lawyers were all permitted and prevalent in the colony.

The population of the state was around 56,071, and more were arriving. There was pressure to make more land available for settlers. At that time, the state did not have the military resources to defend these lands, despite many wanting to open them to white settlements. In 1780, the Georgia legislature

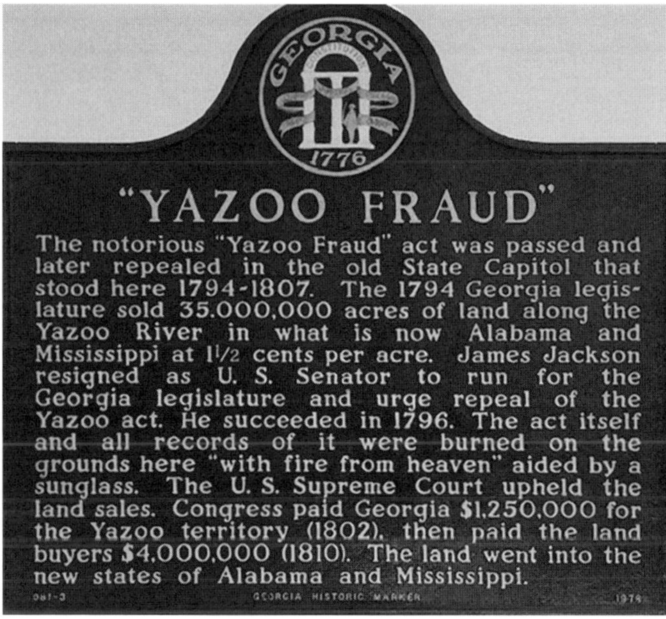

Yazoo Land Fraud marker. *Georgia Historical Society.*

was open to listening to proposals from outside companies that were willing to pay for the right to buy property in these western lands. The state had previously tried, unsuccessfully, to transfer the property to the U.S. Congress.

Mathews convinced the state to pass the Yazoo Act, which transferred thirty-five million acres of land in western territory to four companies. The price of the transfer totaled only $500,000. Gunn then arranged for the $500,000 to be distributed to individual speculators, including himself, state legislators, and state officials, who planned to mark up the price and resell the land to settlers. Left out of the transaction was any money paid to the Native tribes.

As the Yazoo Act moved toward its final passage, citizens rose up in protest. Cries of corruption were leveled against the governor. Street demonstrations and protests were staged against the action of the legislature. But the law was passed anyway and signed by Mathews. The purchase was completed, and state money was transferred to the three private companies.

U.S. Senator James Jackson listened to citizens' concerns and worked to overturn the sale. He used grand jury testimony and local newspaper stories to change the makeup of the next legislative session. Jackson's allies then held hearings that substantiated the corruption charges. In 1796, the new legislature passed legislation. The new governor, Jared Irwin, signed into law a Rescinding Act, which nullified the Yazoo sale.

Those who were part of the sale and tainted by the Yazoo scandal were denied reelection, and in 1798, a state constitutional amendment was passed to prevent any similar action from happening again.

In 1802, Georgia transferred the land and Yazoo claims to the federal government. The United States paid the state of Georgia $1.25 million and agreed to extinguish the remaining claims of Native tribes.

Northern speculators who had purchased land from the original Yazoo companies asked Congress for repayment and sued for redress. In 1810, Chief Justice John Marshall ruled in the case of *Fletcher v. Peck* that the Rescinding Act of 1796 was unconstitutional. In 1814, Congress resolved the issue and paid the speculators $5 million from the proceeds of land sales in the territory. The challenge to the constitutionality of the 1796 act caused a major change in the federal government's relation to state laws. A *New Georgia Encyclopedia* article by Dan Coenen explains why the ruling was so important for the early colonial period.

> *Robert Fletcher, a resident of New Hampshire, had brought his Yazoo tract from John Peck, a resident of Massachusetts, who traced his title back to the State of Georgia through innocent purchases. In connection with the land transfer, Peck promised Fletcher that the title had not been constitutionally imparted by the 1796 rescinding legislation. When that proved not to be the case, Fletcher sued Peck. The case thus entailed Peck arguing to the U.S. Supreme Court that no breach of his promise to Fletcher had occurred.*
>
> *In Chief John Marshall's opinion in the Fletcher case, the Court sustained the constitutional challenge to the Georgia rescinding act, thus showing an important precedent: that the Supreme Court has the power to declare state laws unconstitutional. (The Court's earlier and most famous decision in* Marburg v. Madison *had recognized the Court's ability to strike down acts of the U.S. Congress, without specifically considering the Court's power to invalidate laws enacted by state.)*
>
> Fletcher *is important for other reasons as well. The case laid the basis for the principal that the limitations imposed by the "impairment of contract" clause extend to governmental, as well as private, contractual obligations. Even more important, the courts in the Fletcher case hinted at the notion that Americans may have judicially enforceable rights rooted not so much in the specific language of the U.S. Constitution as in "general principals, which are common to our free institutions." Much of the court's most controversial work ever since has explored the*

> *extent to which the Court may protect human rights that do not find clear expression in the text of the Constitution.*

Later, the land transferred to Congress in 1802 became the states of Alabama and Mississippi. Another legacy of the Yazoo fraud grew out of Native claims for redress, which were not addressed. As more white settlers moved west, the notorious Indian Removal of Act of 1838 allowed President Andrew Jackson to move Creek, Seminole, Choctaw, Chickasaw, and Cherokee tribes out of their homelands to reservations west of the Mississippi River. The Yazoo Land Fraud Act helped spawn the "Trail of Tears." The disgraced governor George Mathews moved to western lands. He was commissioned by President James Madison to lead an expiation in Florida against the Spanish government. The mission failed, and he was recalled by Madison. As Mathews traveled to Washington through Augusta to protest his rejection, he fell ill. He died there in 1812 and was buried at St. Paul Episcopal Church.

26

VIRGINIA HILL

A Mob Queen and Organized Crime Figure

I do not know what they do. I was upstairs because I had allergies from the cactus," said Virginia Hill to a congressional committee.

Marietta native Virginia Hill was a mob queen and an organized crime figure. She was famous for being the wife of mobster Buggy Siegel. Hill was born in Lipscomb, Alabama, in 1916. Her father, Mack Hill, moved to Marietta when she was eight. Hill lived on Church Street near the First Presbyterian Church and attended Roberts Grammar School.

Times were hard in the Great Depression, and at the age of fifteen, Hill dropped out of school to work in a dress shop on the Marietta Square. She was a natural beauty, and boys would visit her during her days off. Her father was a local hoodlum and a terrible drunk who was often heard beating his wife and children, including Hill.

To escape the abuse, in 1931, Hill married a sixteen-year-old boy named George Randell. In 1933, the couple left Marietta and moved to Chicago, where they hoped to find a better life. The city was hosting the "Century of Progress" World's Fair, and Hill found a job there as a server. To earn extra income, she became a sex worker.

Randell and Hill divorced, and she found a new job working at a fair exhibit called the San Carlo Village. The village was a mafia enterprise that promoted gambling and the sale of illegal whiskey in its back room. It was there she met bookmaker Joseph Epstein. He was taken with her beauty and wit and introduced her to what was called the "Chicago Outfit." She became a mistress to many Chicago Outfit bosses and acted as a courier, passing memos and messages to other mob associates. Law enforcement began tracking her and suspected that she was what is called a "clearing house" for organized crime.

Hill became associated with so many men as lovers it would take a computer to track them all. In the 1930s, she was the top model of the underworld. Epstein gave her expensive clothes and jewels. She agreed to target rich men so they'd give her money for favors and nonexistent investments; she'd then deliver the money to Epstein.

She then met Benjamin "Bugsy" Siegel, one of the top mafia bosses in the United States. Because of his violent temper, he was described as "crazy as a big bug." Siegel and Hill quickly became an item. They were a beautiful couple and moved from Chicago to Hollywood, where Siegel had a swanky home in Beverly Hills. He introduced Hill to many of his mob friends, including George Raft, an actor who was famous for appearing in gangster movies. She also met other mob figures, including mafia kingpin Charles "Lucky" Luciano and Mickey Cohen.

One night, Hill got into a fight with another woman she thought was making eyes at Siegel. The fight became a brawl. Police were called, and Hill was arrested. The fight was picked up by national newspapers, which labeled Hill the "Mob Beauty Queen." And this is how she became famous all over the country.

Siegel gave Hill the nickname "Flamingo" for her beautiful legs. In one of his projects in Las Vegas, he named the Flamingo Hotel in her honor. The hotel project was financed by many of his mobster friends. But it ran into construction problems, and costs went over budget. The hotel was budgeted to cost $1.2 million, but its costs had grown to more than $6 million. In typical mob fashion, when someone did not do what was asked of them, trouble followed. Things did not look good for Siegel. On the evening of June 20, 1947, Virginia and Siegel were lounging in her bedroom when a hail of gunfire came through her window, killing Siegel. Siegel's mob friends denied being involved in the murder, but it looked like a typical syndicate hit. His murder has never been solved. The Las Vegas Flamingo Hotel and Casino is still in operation today. Only Virginia Hill knew it was named for her at the time.

Hill later moved back to Marietta to be near her mother, who kept a colt behind her house. Virginia liked to wear shorts and ride the pony around the Marietta Square. One thirteen-year-old boy named Billy Kinney wrote that many boys ran after her just to get a look. She would stop many times to visit with her young admirers. Kinney later became a famous writer for the local newspaper.

Hill moved on and directed drug trafficking out of Mexico; she would send the profits to her Chicago associates. To keep heroin and other drugs moving, she started having an affair with the son of a Mexican finance minister.

Then Hill moved to Hollywood, where she tried to land roles in the movies. She stared a fling with producer Carl Laemmle Jr., heir to a fortune left by his filmmaking father. He fell in love with her, but when he did not find Hill any movie work, she dropped him.

Hill became wealthy by skimming money from the transactions she was conducting for her mafioso associates.

In 1950, Hill traveled to a ski resort in Sun Vally, Idaho, where she met Hans Hauser, an expat from Switzerland. They soon became lovers. He was surprised when he started seeing shady men coming to the resort. They were bringing Hill sacks of $50 and $100 bills to hide from the IRS. The FBI showed up to investigate, and the hotel asked her to leave. Hauser and Hill left and were later married.

Congress became interested in Hill's crime actives. The Kefauver Committee subpoenaed her to question her about some of her associates. She appeared in nationally televised hearings that made her a major crime figure. During the congressional hearings, she denied knowing that any of her friends were racketeers or gang members. She told the committee, "I never knew anything about their business. I do not even understand it." When asked about her and Bugsy Siegel's involvement with the Flamingo Hotel, she said, "I don't know anything about the hotel. I stayed upstairs there because I had allergies from the cactus." Her answer caused committee members to break out into laugher.

The committee excused her, and when she left, she slugged a reporter, Marjorie Farsworth. She told the press, "She hoped an atomic bomb would fall on them." The scene was captured on national television and made her even more famous.

The IRS soon went after her and served a lien on her property for $161,000 in back taxes. Her home, along with two cars, five expensive furs, and ruby and diamond rings were auctioned off. In 1954, a grand jury in Los Angeles indicted her on four counts of tax evasion. The state asked for $227,000 in back taxes and said she would face a year in prison.

Virginia Hill, now Virginia Hauser, moved to Austria with her husband, Hans. She kept her contacts with the "Outfit's" friends in Chicago. Soon,

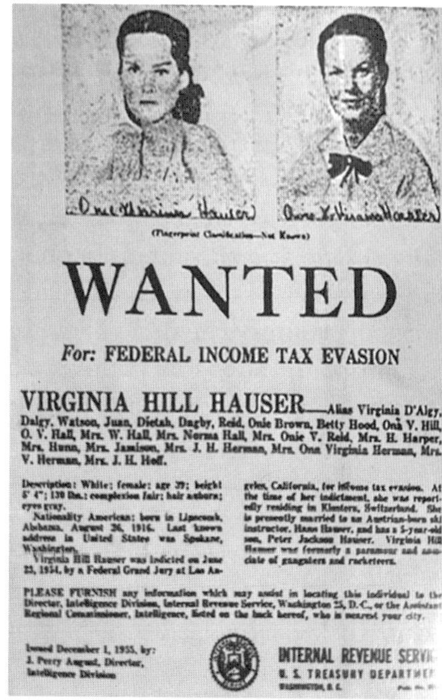

Left: Virginia Hill, "Bugsy's Baby." *Birch Lane Press, 1993.*

Right: Virginia Hill Hauser. *Public domain.*

she was moving money from the United States to Swiss banks for the underworld. She was running out of money, so her old friend Joseph Epstein gave her $100,000 to keep her afloat.

After running away from the law all her life, she wearily told her husband that she wanted to die by suicide. It was not the first time she had tried to end her life. In 1965, her husband had found her near death from a drug overdose in her bedroom. At the time, he rushed her to the hospital to have the drugs pumped from her stomach.

In 1966, Hill-Hauser was out of money. She found an old boyfriend named John Adonis living in Naples, Italy. She went to see Adonis, and according to records, she tried to extort money from him. Some of his associates found her and forced drugs down her throat to kill her. Later, her body was found in her motel room. The police in Naples were controlled by the Mafia, so they could not find any suspects for her murder. She was buried in a cemetery in Salzburg, Austria.

In 1950, Virginia Hill became the movie star she always aspired to be. She was played by Joan Crawford in the movie *The Damned Don't Cry*. She was also the subject of a later movie, in which she's played by Dyan Cannon. In the 1991 movie *Bugsy*, Hill's character is played Annette Bening, with Bugsy Siegel played by Warren Beatty.

For a girl from the small town of Marietta, Virginia Hill led quite a life. As a thirteen-year-old boy, young Billy Kinney had dreamed he would become Hill's boyfriend. Later, he was a famous reporter for the local paper, the *Marietta Daily Journal*, authoring many articles about his conversions with her that were picked up by the Associated Press and published in newspapers across the country, including those in Chicago, Los Angeles, Los Vegas, and Hollywood. It made Hill the most famous "Mob Beauty Queen" in history. Kinney told his readers of the *Marietta Daily Journal*, "I will never forget her!"

27

THE NIGHT STALKER AND THE ATLANTA CHILD MURDERS

Terror in Atlanta

An evil fiend terrorized the city of Atlanta during 1979 and 1980. He was a serial killer who cased the streets looking for children and young people. A special task force of some one hundred agents tried to find him for more than two years. The body count continued until it included thirty children and young adults.

At the time, Atlanta was called the "city too busy to hate" and was the home of the "world's busiest airport." The city was the most progressive in the South and was the home of Dr. Martin L. King Jr. The killing spree was a distressing event for the city, which prided itself as the epicenter of the civil rights movement. The city was terrified, and Mayor Maynard Jackson, city officials, and police cautioned children to stay in their homes and not go outside after dark. Young people named the killer the "Night Stalker." They were fearful of being caught and killed.

On July 28, 1979, a woman was walking near a nonresidential area of the city when she spotted the partial remains of two Black children. The woman called the police and pointed out her horrific discovery. The victims were identified as Edward H. Smith, fourteen, and Alfred James Evan, thirteen. Their distraught parents were found, and they told the police they thought their children had gone to the movies.

As summer passed, the mother of Milton Harvey, fourteen, reported him missing. She had sent him on an errand on his bicycle, but he never returned. His body was found in the woods near a four-lane road near East Point. Atlanta's Missing Persons Unit worked to find whether the murder was connected to their earlier double-homicide case.

On Sunday, October 21, 1979, Yusuf Bell, nine, went to a grocery store to buy items for a friend. He never returned. A man was walking by an abandoned school when he found the body of a young Black child and called the police. Bell was killed about a mile from his home.

It became clear that the murders were connected, and Mayor Jackson formed a task force to deal with the crisis. Yet the killings kept occurring. In March 1980, the body of Angel Laurier, twelve, was discovered. On March 11, 1980, Jeffrey Mathis, ten, was found. Eric Antonio Middlebrooks, fourteen, added to the body count.

The murders were happening more often, which caused people to wonder whether the nightmare would ever end. The mayor's task force expanded to include state and federal police and the FBI. Their normal techniques were not finding the killer, so more unorthodox methods were used. This included asking Jean Dixon and other astrologers and psychics to try to find the person responsible.

Photos of Atlanta's missing children. *Atlanta Journal, April 2, 1980.*

The Associated Press

Wayne Williams, now 47 and serving a life sentence, was blamed for 24 of 29 murders of young black boys and men.

AJC CONTINUING COVERAGE
ATLANTA CHILD MURDERS

Williams offers help to uncover 'truth'

Convicted murderer has said he's innocent in child killings case.

By Joshua Sharpe
jsharpe@ajc.com

Wayne Williams, the long-accused Atlanta Child Murders suspect, released a statement Monday morning saying he was pleased that officials are taking a new look at old evidence in the killings.

Williams, 60, has long maintained his innocence in the killing of 29 black children and young adults murdered around the city four decades ago. He is serving two life sentences for the murders of two adults but was never charged with the other slayings.

"I stand fully ready and willing to cooperate with any renewed investigation to find the truth on what happened with the purpose of straightening up any lies and misconceptions of my unjust convictions," he said in a statement read in a news conference by Dewayne Hendrix of the Wayne Williams Freedom Project.

The statement comes just weeks after Mayor Keisha Lance Bottoms announced that authorities would attempt to use new technology to test evidence in the cases, such as DNA and fibers.

Wayne Williams, serving two life sentences, is "fully ready and willing to cooperate with any renewed investigation." AJC 1991

Williams continued on B6

Wayne Williams. *Atlanta Journal.*

Yet on and on the killer went. Month by month, the horrors were relentless until a new, older victim was found. A Black man, Eddie Duncan, twenty-one, was found in a stream near the Chattahoochee River the day after another victim was pulled from the river at about the same location. Next was Michael McIntosh, twenty-three, whose body was found next to the same river.

The Special Task Force of the FBI began a "bridge surveillance" effort whereby certain selected bridges across the Chattahoochee River would be placed under physical surveillance overnight. The body count had risen to include twenty-nine victims with no end in sight.

During the evening of May 21, 1981, officer R.E. Campbell was stationed near a bridge in Cobb County when heard a large splash. He saw car headlights driving at the top end of the bridge. The car drove to a liquor store, where police pulled over the driver, a Black man named Wayne Bertram Williams. He was dressed in a dark shirt and slacks and was wearing a baseball cap. He responded, "I know—it's about those boys, isn't it?"

The splash at the river was the break in the case and was known in the local media as the "splash heard around the world." The victim in the

The Atlanta Child Murders: The Night Stalker, by Jack Mallard.

river was Nathaniel Carter, twenty-eight. Carter, like most of the victims, had died of asphyxia due to strangulation.

Williams was arrested and charged with the murders of Carter and Jimmy Ray Payne. Williams was not charged with the deaths of the other victims because even when prosecutors know someone is guilty, if there is no evidence, they cannot prosecute. But suddenly, after Williams was arrested, the murders stopped.

After a lengthy trial, Willams was found guilty of the two murders as charged and was sentenced to two life terms.

The parents of the other murdered children have wondered: Why abruptly close their cases? The unsatisfying end has led to questions, doubts, anger, and rumors. These parents are still grief-stricken and, sadly, still searching for answers. At the time of this writing, Williams is sixty years old and is still in Telfair County State Prison. Williams still claims he is innocent.

BIBLIOGRAPHY

Anderson, William. *The Wild Man from Sugar Creek: The Political Career of Eugene Talmadge.* Louisiana State University Press, 1975.

Associated Press. "Antifreeze Killer Lynn Turner Dies in Prison." August 31, 2010.

Atlanta History Center. "Marvin Griffin." www.atlantahistory.com.

Barnes, Margaret Anne. *Murder in Coweta County.* Pelican Publishing, 1976.

Baron, Elizabeth R. *Longstreet: The Confederate General Who Defied the South.* Simon & Schuster, 2023.

Bolton, Philip. "Pair Extradited for Murder Trial." *Macon Telegraph,* November 7, 1974.

Borneman, Walter R. *1812: The War of 1812.* HarperCollins, 2004.

Bradwell, Joe. "Doc Holliday Stories." *Valdosta Daily Times,* n.d.

Burch, Audra D.S. "Who Killed Atlanta's Children?" *New York Times,* April 30, 2019.

Canford, Peter G. *Damnation Hospital.* Old Capital Press, 2009.

Carter, Larry. *Polk County, Georgia: The First One Hundred Years.* N.p., 2012.

Christie's. "Forbes Collection of American Historical Documents: Gwinnett, Button (1735–1777)." https://www.christies.com/.

Cobb, James C. *Georgia Odyssey, A Short History of the State.* 1997. Reprint, University of Georgia Press, 2008.

Coenen, Dan. "Fletcher v. Peck." *New Georgia Encyclopedia.* June 6, 2017. https://www.georgiaencyclopedia.org/.

Connelly, Thomas L., and Barbara L. Bellows. *God and General Longstreet.* Louisiana State University Press, 1982.

Davidson, Andy. "The Dodge Land Wars: A History of Violence." CrimeReads. October 12, 2022. https://crimereads.com/.

Deborah. "Moore's Ford: The Nation's Last Mass Lynching." University Libraries, University of Georgia. Submitted on Wednesday, July 25, 2018. https://www.libs.uga.edu/.

Dillman, Caroline. "Deportation of Roswell Women." *New Georgia Encyclopedia*. August 20, 2013. https://www.georgiaencyclopedia.org/.

Ebel, Carol. "George Mathews." *New Georgia Encyclopedia*. September 11, 2014. https://www.georgiaencyclopedia.org/.

Edmonds, Andy. *Bugsy's Baby. The Secrets Life of Mob Queen Virginia Hill*. Birch Lane Press, 1993.

Elliott, Mary, and Hughes, Jazmine. "The 1619 Project: We've Got to Tell the Unvarnished Truth." *New York Times*, August 18, 2019.

Encyclopaedia Britannia. "United States History: Prohibition." April 5, 2025. https://www.britannica.com/.

Equal Justice Initiative. "A History of Racial Injustice: White Mob Lynches Two Black Couples in Walton County, Georgia." https://eji.org/news/tag/history-of-racial-injustice/.

Feldman, Christopher. "Moonshine Wars Make the Cover." *Harper's Weekly*, November 2, 1978. *North Georgia History*. www.northgeorgiahistory.com.

FindLaw. "Turner v. State, Decided: February 26, 2007." https://caselaw.findlaw.com/.

Fort Frederica National Monument Georgia. "Igbo Landing." National Park Service. https://www.nps.gov/.

Freeman, David B. *Carved in Stone: The History of Stone Mountain*. Mercer University Press, 1997.

Freeman, Douglas Southhall. *Lee's Lieutenants*. Charles Scribner's Sons, 1944.

Galphin, Bruce. *The Riddle of Lester Maddox*. Camelot Publishers, 1968.

Georgia Historical Society. Moore's Ford Lynching marker. Erected 1999.

Google Arts & Culture. "Daily Life at Andersonville Prison." https://artsandculture.google.com/.

Green, Melissa Fay. *Praying for Sheetrock*. Addison-Wesley Publishers, 1991.

———. *The Temple Bombing*. Da Capo Press, 2006.

Griffin, D.W., dir. *The Birth of a Nation*. David W. Griffith Corp., 1915. (Landmark silent film.)

Groom, Winston. *Patriotic Fire: Andrew Jackson and Jean Laffitte at the Battle of New Orleans*. Knopf Doubleday, 2006.

Harper, Houston R. "The Revenge of John Prior." *Rome News-Tribune*, April 18, 1897.

Harvey, Steve. "Mrs. Machetti's Parole Request Denied by Panel." *Atlanta Journal-Constitution*, January 4, 1984.

History of American Women. https://www.womenhistoryblog.com/.

Hughes, Brad. "The Alday Murders." *Early County News*, May 9, 2023.

Jackson, Olin. *Georgia's Doc Holliday*. Whippoorwill Publications, 2006.

Johnson, Nicole. *Sapelo Island's Hog Hammock/Michele.* Arcadia Publishing, 2009.
Kantor, MacKinlay. *Andersonville.* World Publishing Company, 1955. (Winner of the Pulitzer Prize in 1956.)
Kennedy, Jackie. "Touring 'Murder in Coweta County.'" *Newnan-Coweta Magazine*, March/April 2023.
King James Bible Dictionary. "Blacker: A Vulgar Term Applied to a Mean Fellow, Who Treats Others with Foul Abuse." https://kingjamesbibledictionary.com/.
Kovac, Joe, Jr. "Rebecca Machetti, Sentenced to Death For 1974 Macon Murder Plot, Dies of Covid-19." *Macon Telegraph*, September 16, 2020.
Lamplugh, Georgia R. "Yazoo Land Fraud." *New Georgia Encyclopedia.* June 8, 2017. https://www.georgiaencyclopedia.org/.
Leerhsen, Charles. "Who Was Ty Cobb? The History We Know That Is Wrong." *Imprimis Magazine* 45, no. 3 (March 2016).
Lisby, Gregory. *Julian Harris and the Columbus Enquirer-Sun: Consequences of Winning the Pulitzer Prize.* Association for Education in Journalism and Mass Communication, January 1988.
Longstreet, James. *From Manassas to Appomattox*. Philadelphia, 1896.
Mallard, Jack. *The Atlanta Child Murders: The Night Stalker*. Self-published, 2009.
Mann, Charles C. *1491: New Revelations of the America Before Columbus.* Vintage Books, 2006.
Martin, Douglas. "J.B. Stoner, 81, Fervent Racist and Benchmark for Extremism, Dies." *New York Times*, April 29, 2005.
Martin, Roland. "Igbo Landing, Historic Site, St. Simons Island, Georgia." *Encyclopaedia Britannica*. https://www.britannica.com/.
Mathis, George. "America's Last Slave Ship Landed in Georgia." *Atlanta Journal-Constitution*, January 31, 2017.
Miller, Zell. *Great Georgians*. Vol. 25. *1733–1983*. Advocate Press, 1983.
Mob Museum. "Benjamin 'Bugsy' Siegel." https://admission.themobmuseum.org/.
———. "Virginia Hill." https://admission.themobmuseum.org/.
Monroe, Kristopher. "Historian Uncovered Illegal Slave-Traders' Dubious Dealings." *Savannah Now*, March 17, 2018.
National Park Service. "Andersonville: National Prisoner of War Museum." December 6, 2022. www.nps.gov.
Nelson, Gary, dir. *Murder in Coweta County*. Telecom Entertainment, 1983.
Payne, David H. "Central State Hospital." *New Georgia Encyclopedia*. March 2, 2022. https://www.georgiaencyclopedia.org/.
PBS. "Andersonville, National Historic Site, Georgia: Captain Henry Wirz, Today Few Civil War Figures Are as Controversial as Henry Wirz." https://www.pbs.org/.
———. "Henry Wirz, Confederate War Criminal." Georgia Historical Society. https://www.pbs.org/.

Pearce, Al, et al. *NASCAR 75 Years*. Motorbooks, 2023.

Pomerania, Gary M. *Where Peachtree Meets Sweet Auburn*. Scribner, 1996.

Riggall, Hunter. "Nonprofits Ask for Help Tracking Homeless Crisis." *Marietta Daily Journal*, June 14–15, 2025.

Rohrer, Katherine E. "Wanderer." *New Georgia Encyclopedia*. September 24, 2020. https://www.georgiaencyclopedia.org/.

Sargent, Gordon D. "A North Georgia Journal of History: Volume III." *Rome News-Tribune*, 1897.

Savage, Randall. "Maree Tells of Murder." *Macon News*. January 29, 1973.

Shaara, Michael. *The Killer Angels: The Classic Novel of the Civil War*. Ballentine Books, 1975.

Shipp, Bill. *Murder at Broad River Bridge: The Slaying of Lemuel Penn by the Ku Klux Klan*. Peachtree Publishing, 1981.

Smith, Gordon Burns. "Georgia's Signers of the Declaration of Independence." 2009. https://gasocietysar.org/. (Published with permission of the estate.)

Smith, Halle. "Involved from the Start: Georgia's Role in in America's Birth." Edited by Tiffany Harte. Atlanta History Center. July 3, 2024. https://www.atlantahistorycenter.com/.

Stratham, Frances Patton. *The Roswell Women*. Arrow, 1987.

Swaine, Jon. "FBI Investigates Claim Suspects in 1945 Georgia Mass Lynching May Be Alive." *Guardian*, February 16, 2015. https://www.theguardian.com/.

Talmadge, Herman E., and Mark Royden Winchell. *Talmadge: A Political Legacy, a Politician's Life: A Memoir*. Peachtree Publishing, 1987.

Thompson, Neal. *Driving With the Devil: Southern Moonshine, Detroit Wheels, and the Birth of NASCAR*. Crown Publishing Group, 2007.

Thurmond, Georgia E. "Mill Women Monument." Photograph.

University of Georgia, Special Collection Library.

Vigdor, Neil. "Records in 1946 Lynching Case Must Remain Sealed, Court Rules." *New York Times*, March 30, 2020.

Walls, Jim. "Daughters Describe Attempt to Kill." *Atlanta Journal-Constitution*, July 22, 1983.

———. "Retrial of Machetti Begins in Gwinnett." *Atlanta Journal-Constitution*, July 20, 1983.

Weldon White, Jaclyn. *Pure Evil: The Machetti Murders of Macon, Georgia*. Mercer University Press, 2020.

Wexler, Laura. *Fire in a Canebrake: The Last Mass Lynching in America*. Scribner, 2013.

Wikipedia. "Lynn Turner (murderer)." https://www.wikipedia.org/.

Young, Neely. "The Dodge Land Troubles." *Georgia Trend*, March 1, 2013.

ABOUT THE AUTHOR

Neely Young is a native of Cedartown, Georgia, a graduate of the University of Georgia, and a proud journalist. In 1968, he joined his family-owned newspaper, the *Valdosta Daily Times*, working in the photography department. After leaving Valdosta, he worked in various positions as both an editor and publisher for newspapers in Canton, Dalton, and Clayton County. In 1986, he became the CEO of Morris Newspaper Corporation, which owned and ran forty newspapers in six states.

Three years later, he formed Southern Newspaper Company with Tom Cousins, building a chain of thirteen newspapers over nine years. In 1998, Southern Publishing was sold to Community Newspapers Holdings. The following year, Young, along with Cousins, bought *Georgia Trend* magazine, a publication with a circulation of fifty thousand that has become the state's go-to source for business, political, and development information. Young served as the magazine's publisher and editor-in-chief for eighteen years until his retirement in 2017.

Young served as a curator for the Georgia Historical Society and often wrote about historical figures in his columns for *Georgia Trend* magazine. In 2021, he wrote *Georgia Made*, a book containing individual profiles of the most influential Georgians in the twentieth century. For writing the book, he was nominated for the Georgia Author of the Year Award. This second book, *Notorious Georgia*, is a series of profiles of evil men, women, and institutions and the people who brought them to justice.